# MASTER SUDOKU

**By Jack Cecil, Jr.**

*Explore the intricacies of Sudoku*

Dedicated to my fantastic children Samuel, Isaac, and Cara, and to my
Mom and Dad, JoAnne and Jack (Mammy & Pappy Yokum)

Edited by: Kristin Gillenwater
Cover by: Bree Bridges


Thanks to Margie Templeton for the line editing.

*AuthorHouse™*
*1663 Liberty Drive*
*Bloomington, IN 47403*
*www.authorhouse.com*
*Phone: 1-800-839-8640*

*First published by AuthorHouse 1/25/2010*

*ISBN: 978-1-4490-0276-3(sc)*

*Printed in the United States of America*
*Bloomington, Indiana*

*This book is printed on acid-free paper.*

# MASTER SUDOKU

## Introduction

As a field engineer, business consultant, and construction project manager, it seems as though my entire life has revolved around problem solving. Even in my free time, I enjoy mathematics and recreational puzzle solving.

Over the past few years, I've become enamored with Sudoku puzzles. After working several puzzles and becoming frustrated with the slow process of solving them through trial and error, I wondered if there was a systematic way to work these little beasts that would effectively speed up an otherwise tedious activity. Or, at least, save me a lot of frustration.

After many hours of analysis I developed a systematic method, which accelerates the ability to solve a Sudoku puzzle compared to the old trial and error method. Granted, trial and error will be necessary to a certain extent, but my methods reduce the time required to solve these little monsters and, consequently, reduce the frustration of Sudoku puzzle solving.

In this book you will learn how to analyze these puzzles, what to look for when "attacking" a puzzle, and how to dramatically reduce your solving time by selecting the right starting point.

If you are a seasoned Sudoku player, brush up on the fundamentals in the first part of the book and then concentrate mainly on the *Speed Sudoku* and *Creating Your Own Sudoku* sections

As you can see below, a Sudoku puzzle is comprised of 81 small squares or **cells**, which is then divided into 9 larger squares. All 81 squares must be filled in so that each larger square or **box**, each row, and each column contain the digits 1 through 9. The digits are never duplicated. Therefore, there never is more than one 9 or one 6, for example, in any row, column or box.

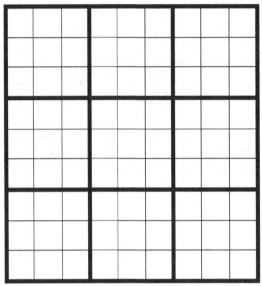

Figure 1.0

At the outset, you will notice in a regular Sudoku puzzle that 20 to 40 of the 81 cells have already been filled in with a digit ranging from 1 to 9. We will call these filled in cells *given clues*, also called **hard clues**. Each of the given clues becomes an integral part of the puzzle solving process.

## Why Solve Puzzles?

For most of us, a great part of life consists of solving problems. Whether we are students or workers, retired, young or old, our problem-solving acumen is directly proportional to mental skills, such as logic, perspicacity, patience, powers of observation, data gathering, skills, memory, and concentration. Solving puzzles of all types facilitates and actually improves these mental skills so that we can be more effective problem solvers in real life situations.

Research has proven that puzzle solving and other mentally challenging activities can enhance and even improve mental function.

> *There is no expedient to which man will not resort to avoid the real labor of thinking.*
>
> - Sir Joshua Reynolds (1723-1792)

This quotation hung on the wall of our business office for almost fifty years and is indelibly etched into my mind. You can witness the accuracy of this quotation everywhere you look, from the popularity of mindless movies and music to the continued decline in the number of hours per capita people spend reading or pursuing other mentally enriching interests. Puzzle solving is a wonderful way to enhance and increase mental capacity and concentration—activities which are invaluable in successful living.

## Getting Started

In beginning to solve a puzzle, it is helpful to determine the weaknesses in the puzzle and to attack its weakest point. This is especially true when working on the easier Sudoku puzzles such as the one on the next page.

Remember, the more given clues in a puzzle, generally speaking, the easier it is to solve. If a puzzle has thirty-six given clues, that means it is a relatively easy puzzle. In order to solve this critter, employ elementary logic or a system I call *Solve the Simple Square*, or **S.S.S.**

Listed below are some basic terms used in this guide to refer to different parts of a Sudoku puzzle.

**Cell** – One of the 81 squares in a Sudoku puzzle.
**Box** – One of the nine larger sections of a Sudoku puzzle. Each box contains nine cells.
**Column** – There are nine columns. Each column contains nine cells.
**Row** – There are nine rows. Each row contains nine cells.

## Solve the Simple Square

Begin with the large box that contains the most given clues. Since all of the large boxes in Figure 2.1 contain the same number of clues, begin in the upper left hand corner and the first empty cell in the top row.

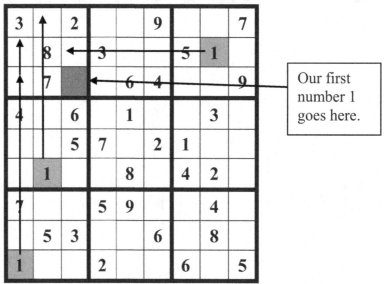

Figure 2.1

The numbers 3, 2, 8 and 7 are given in the upper lefthand box. The missing numbers are 1, 4, 5, 6 and 9. Notice that 1's have been placed as given clues in the large boxes below the target box and the large box in the upper right hand corner. This leaves only one option for placing the 1 in the top left-hand box. See Figure 2.2 below.

Our first number 1 goes here.

Figure 2.2

Since the cell in the lower right hand corner of our target box is the only possible place the 1 will fit within the Sudoku rules, this cell is a *solid "1."* Use this number as a solid clue to help us solve the other cells.

Next, find the spot for the next missing number in the box in the upper left hand corner, the 4. Notice Figure 2.3 has two possible locations for the number 4 based on the clues given, so place a small number 4 in both of them.

| 3 | 4 | 2 |   |   | 9 |   |   | 7 |
|---|---|---|---|---|---|---|---|---|
| ↑ | 8 | 4 | 3 |   |   | 5 | 1 |   |
|   | 7 | 1 |   | 6 | 4 |   |   | 9 |
| 4 |   | 6 |   | 1 |   |   | 3 |   |
|   |   | 5 | 7 |   | 2 | 1 |   |   |
|   | 1 |   |   | 8 |   | 4 | 2 |   |
| 7 |   |   | 5 | 9 |   |   | 4 |   |
|   | 5 | 3 |   |   | 6 |   | 8 |   |
| 1 |   |   | 2 |   |   | 6 |   | 5 |

Figure 2.3

These small number 4's indicate that it is possible, at this point in solving this particular puzzle, that the 4 could go in either cell but in none of the remaining seven cells. These little 4's are *soft clues*. The soft clues will become instrumental in helping solve more complex Sudoku puzzles.

**Types of Clues**

At this point, let's discuss the various types of clues and how to use them to solve a Sudoku puzzle.

First, the *given clues* are the number filled cells already given.

Secondly, the hard or *solid clues* are the numbers previously filled, which can be placed nowhere else in the grid.

Thirdly, *soft clues* are also derived during the puzzle solving process. These are the numbers which could be placed possibly in several places and are instrumental in narrowing the possible locations for the solid clues. In the puzzles they are shown as the small numbers.

In order to reach a solution, convert the soft clues into solid clues. Manage this by filling in more and more cells around the cells containing the soft clues. As the degree of difficulty of the Sudoku puzzles increase, so will the use of soft clues. Many times the cells are filled in with more than one soft clue. Through using logic and the techniques covered later in the book, solving the solid numbers will become a simple process of elimination.

In Figure 2.4 below a solid 1 and two soft 4's are place in the cells. Now, work on the 5. This is found very easily by using the same logic applied when the cell containing the 1 was found.

The 5 missing from this box can only go here.

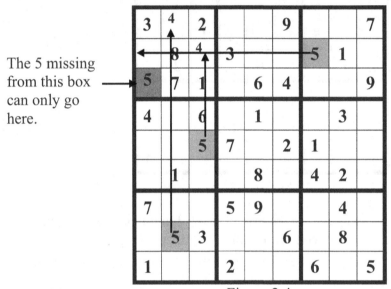

Figure 2.4

Apply elementary logic to discover the only possible place the 5 can go in the upper left hand box is in the lower left hand cell.

Now attempt to place the 6 in the upper left hand box. Because the 'given' 6's have been placed in adjacent cells, the 6 could possibly fit in either of the two cells where 'soft' 6's are placed. See Figure 2.5 below.

| 3 | 4 6 | 2 |   |   | 9 |   |   | 7 |
|---|---|---|---|---|---|---|---|---|
| 6 | 8 | 4 | 3 |   |   | 5 | 1 |   |
| 5 | 7 | 1 |   | 6 | 4 |   |   | 9 |
| 4 |   | 6 |   | 1 |   |   | 3 |   |
|   |   | 5 | 7 |   | 2 | 1 |   |   |
|   | 1 |   |   | 8 |   | 4 | 2 |   |
| 7 |   |   | 5 | 9 |   |   | 4 |   |
|   | 5 | 3 |   |   | 6 |   | 8 |   |
| 1 |   |   | 2 |   |   | 6 |   | 5 |

Figure 2.5

Since 7 and 8 are already given in the upper left hand box, place two soft 9's in the two cells where the 9 could possibly end up being placed in the final solution. See Figure 2.6 below.

| 3 | 4 6 | 2 |   |   | 9 |   |   | 7 |
|---|---|---|---|---|---|---|---|---|
| 6 9 | 8 | 4 9 | 3 |   |   | 5 | 1 |   |
| 5 | 7 | 1 |   | 6 | 4 |   |   | 9 |
| 4 |   | 6 |   | 1 |   |   | 3 |   |
|   |   | 5 | 7 |   | 2 | 1 |   |   |
|   | 1 |   |   | 8 |   | 4 | 2 |   |
| 7 |   |   | 5 | 9 |   |   | 4 |   |
|   | 5 | 3 |   |   | 6 |   | 8 |   |
| 1 |   |   | 2 |   |   | 6 |   | 5 |

Figure 2.6

Now move to the upper middle box. Notice that the 1 can only be placed in the upper left hand corner. Therefore, put a hard 1 in this box. See figure 2.7 on the next page.

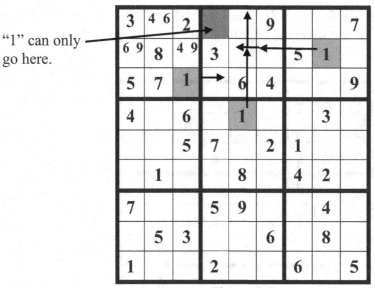

"1" can only go here.

Figure 2.7

Next, using the same logic, place a hard 2 in the center cell. See Figure 2.8 below.

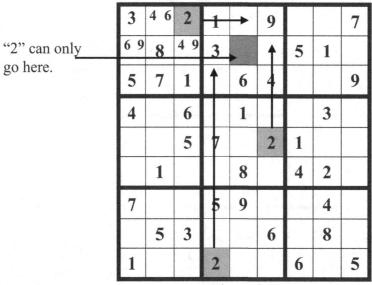

"2" can only go here.

Figure 2.8

It is imperative to be careful when placing the hard numbers—especially when the hard numbers support or replace the soft numbers. Mistakes made in the early part of the puzzle make it extremely difficult to complete without encountering the infamous "Bird's Nest."

| | | |
|---|---|---|
| 4 5 7 1 | 9 | 5 1 |
| 4   7 | 5   7 | 3 |
| 6 | 8 | 2 |

## Reading the Soft Clue

Placed in the large cell above are a series of soft clues in conjunction with the hard clues 9, 3, 6, 8 and 2. In the upper left hand cell the soft clues of 4, 5, 7 and 1 have been placed. In the left center cell 4 and 7 have been placed.

Because the soft 4's are located in the same column and no other soft clues of the number 4 occur in this box, the soft 4's will be helpful in determining the numbers in the same column in the adjoining boxes in the complete Sudoku puzzle.

The same technique with the soft 1's which occur in the same horizontal row can be used. These will be useful in determining placement in the same row in the complete Sudoku puzzle. The soft 4's and soft 1's mentioned above are called **pointing pairs**.

The soft numbers 5 and 7 are not as useful because they are not isolated to one row or column. Look for soft clues isolated to one row or column. This technique is a vital tool in solving Sudoku puzzles and is known as *Pointing Pairs*.

# The Technique of "Listing"

One of the greatest tools for beginners when solving Sudoku puzzles is the Listing Technique. List the clues, which directly affect the box presently being solved. Start by listing the hard clues and then listing the clues in horizontal rows and vertical columns, which immediately affect the cell in question.

This technique is useful not only for beginners, but also can be extremely useful in overcoming difficult snags in Bird's Nest situations.

Try the following example of how to use this technique by going back to the earlier puzzle.

The hard clues 3, 2, 8, 5, 7 and 1 in the upper left box are given as well as a couple of soft clues, 4 and 6 in the top middle cell, 6 and 9 in the middle left cell and 4 and 9 in the middle right cell.

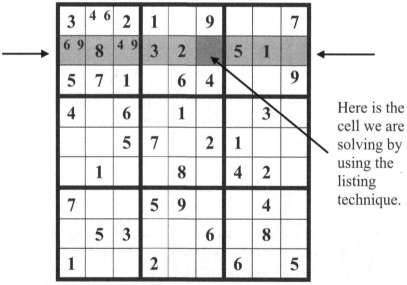

Here is the cell we are solving by using the listing technique.

Figure 3.0

In the upper middle box we have solid clues 1, 9, 3, 2, 6 and 4. The listing technique will be used now to solve the remaining small cells in the upper middle box, starting with the marked cell in Figure 3.0 above.

Begin by listing the hard clues within the upper middle box, which are either given clues or hard clues already solved. On a scrap of paper write 1, 9, 3, 2, 6 and 4:

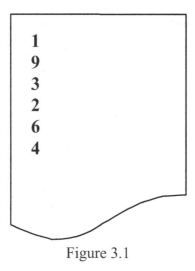

Figure 3.1

Now list the solid clues in the horizontal row you are trying to solve (marked with arrows and shading in Figure 3)—8, 3, 2, 5 and 1:

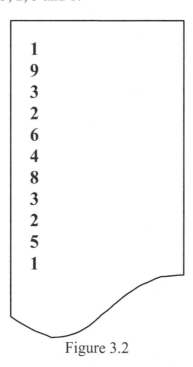

Figure 3.2

In the vertical column affecting the targeted cell being solved are the numbers 6 and 2. See the shaded column in Figure 3.1 below:

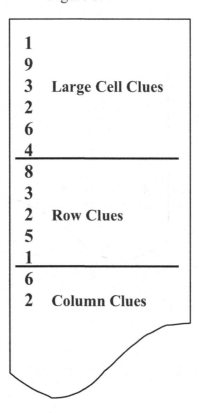

| 3 | <sup>4 6</sup> 2 | 1 |  | 9 |  |  | 7 |
|---|---|---|---|---|---|---|---|

Figure 3.3

Add these numbers to the list, as shown below.

Figure 3.4

<table>
<tr><td>1</td><td></td></tr>
<tr><td>9</td><td></td></tr>
<tr><td>3</td><td>Large Cell Clues</td></tr>
<tr><td>2</td><td></td></tr>
<tr><td>6</td><td></td></tr>
<tr><td>4</td><td></td></tr>
<tr><td>8</td><td></td></tr>
<tr><td>3</td><td></td></tr>
<tr><td>2</td><td>Row Clues</td></tr>
<tr><td>5</td><td></td></tr>
<tr><td>1</td><td></td></tr>
<tr><td>6</td><td></td></tr>
<tr><td>2</td><td>Column Clues</td></tr>
</table>

The list is now completed. The list created contains all the numbers which *cannot* logically be placed in the small cell we are solving.

Now comes the fun part. Start by counting from one to nine on the list containing 1, 2, 3, 4, 5, 6, 8 and 9. Note that 7 is missing. Therefore, the only possible number to place in the small cell being solved is 7.

Although you probably could have solved this particular example without using the Listing Technique, it can be a valuable tool in more complex solving situations.

## Let's Get Started!

Now we are going to solve some puzzles. We will begin with Puzzle 1.

Cut out the blank grid worksheet on the next page. Using a pencil with a good eraser, follow along step by step filling in the numbers on your worksheet.

14

## Worksheet for Puzzle 1

Cut along the dotted line to remove the worksheet.

| | 1 | | 3 | | 6 | | 9 | |
|---|---|---|---|---|---|---|---|---|
| 8 | 7 | | | | 4 | 2 | 1 | 6 |
| | 5 | 6 | | | | 7 | | |
| 3 | 9 | | | 2 | | | | 4 |
| | | | 5 | | 9 | | | |
| 2 | | | | 4 | | | 8 | 5 |
| | | 9 | | | | 8 | 6 | |
| 6 | 3 | 7 | 8 | | | | 5 | 9 |
| | 4 | | 6 | | 7 | | 3 | |

## Puzzle 1

Now begin working through the sample puzzles.

Cut out the worksheet for Puzzle 1 and follow each step until you get to page 21.

The first four sample puzzles will contain a maximum of seven steps per grid, so that the process will appear as simple as possible. Follow in order steps A through G. Remember, solving a Sudoku puzzle is a progressive process. The solution being attempted depends on the prior cells filled in. In other words, step D many times depends on steps A, B and C.

---

**Note:** Always refer to previous grids to verify open cells.

---

This is a fairly easy puzzle with 36 given clues.

Grid 1

| | A | B | C | D | E | F | G | H | I | |
|---|---|---|---|---|---|---|---|---|---|---|
| | | 1 | | 3 | | 6 | | 9 | | 1 |
| | 8 | 7 | | | | 4 | 2 | 1 | 6 | 2 |
| | | 5 | 6 | | | | 7 | | | 3 |
| | 3 | 9 | | | 2 | | | | 4 | 4 |
| | | | | 5 | | 9 | | | | 5 |
| | 2 | | | | 4 | | | 8 | 5 | 6 |
| | | | 9 | | | | 8 | 6 | | 7 |
| | 6 | 3 | 7 | 8 | | | | 5 | 9 | 8 |
| | | 4 | | 6 | | 7 | | 3 | | 9 |

(A) Begin by filling in the soft clues in the puzzle by using the given clues and elementary logic. Notice each column has been marked with the letters A through I and each row with the numbers 1 through 9, allowing easy identification of a particular cell, column or row in the puzzle in order to follow each step.

Because Column A contains a 2 and Row 2 contains a 2, the only possible location for a 2 in the large upper left box is in cell C-1. We say this cell 'must be a 2.'

Puzzle 1 Grid 2

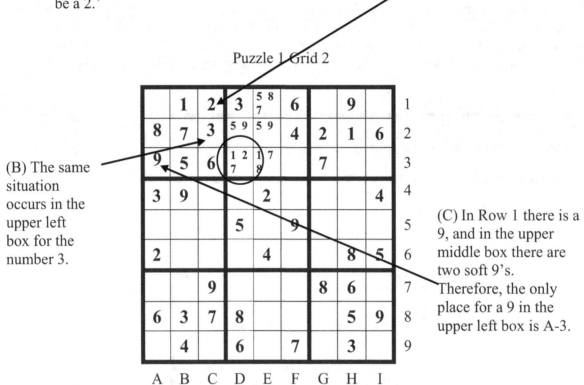

(B) The same situation occurs in the upper left box for the number 3.

(C) In Row 1 there is a 9, and in the upper middle box there are two soft 9's. Therefore, the only place for a 9 in the upper left box is A-3.

## Using "Can Be, Can't Be"

A critical solving tool in placing soft clues as well as solid clues is the 'can be, can't be' method. You will use this method repeatedly in solving sudoku puzzles no matter what level of player you become. For example, in the circled cell above, your inner dialogue might go like this:

"This cell can be 1 (place a soft 1), can be 2 (place a soft 2), can't be 3, 4, 5, 6, can be 7 (place a soft 7), can't be 8 or 9."

The 'can be, can't be' method is one of the greatest solving tools you can use!

## Grid 2

| | A | B | C | D | E | F | G | H | I | |
|---|---|---|---|---|---|---|---|---|---|---|
| 1 | | 1 | 2 | 3 | 5 8 7 | 6 | | 9 | | 1 |
| 2 | 8 | 7 | 3 | 5 9 | 5 9 | 4 | 2 | 1 | 6 | 2 |
| 3 | 9 | 5 | 6 | 1 2 7 | 1 7 8 | | 7 | | | 3 |
| 4 | 3 | 9 | | | 2 | | | | 4 | 4 |
| 5 | | | | 5 | | 9 | | | | 5 |
| 6 | 2 | | | | 4 | | | 8 | 5 | 6 |
| 7 | | | 9 | | | | 8 | 6 | | 7 |
| 8 | 6 | 3 | 7 | 8 | | | | 5 | 9 | 8 |
| 9 | | 4 | | 6 | | 7 | | 3 | | 9 |

A B C D E F G H I

## Puzzle 1 Grid 3

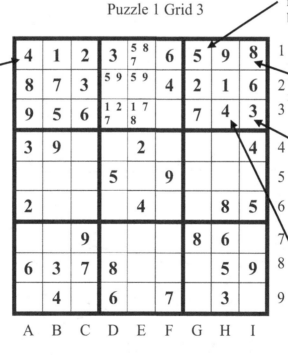

(E) Must be a 5 because it is the only number needed to complete the box. Go to next page.

(B) Row 2 already contains a 4 so the only location for a 4 in this box is cell A-1.

(D) Since there are 8's in Column G & H. Cell I-1 must be an 8.

(A) Because Rows 1 and 2 contain 3's and Column H contains a 3, the only location for a 3 in the upper right hand box is in cell I-3.

(C) Has to be a 4 because Rows 1 & 2 already have 4's.

19

Grid 3

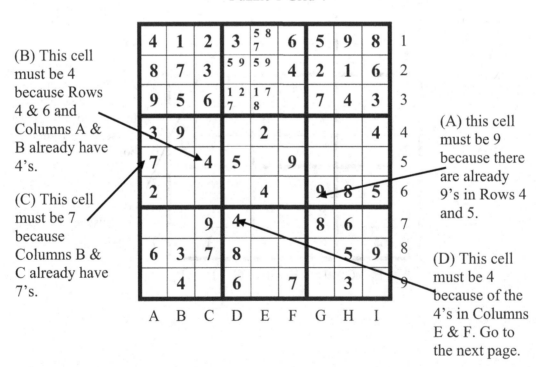

Now the upper left and right boxes are complete so move on to the middle left and right boxes.

Puzzle 1 Grid 4

(B) This cell must be 4 because Rows 4 & 6 and Columns A & B already have 4's.

(C) This cell must be 7 because Columns B & C already have 7's.

(A) this cell must be 9 because there are already 9's in Rows 4 and 5.

(D) This cell must be 4 because of the 4's in Columns E & F. Go to the next page.

20

Grid 4

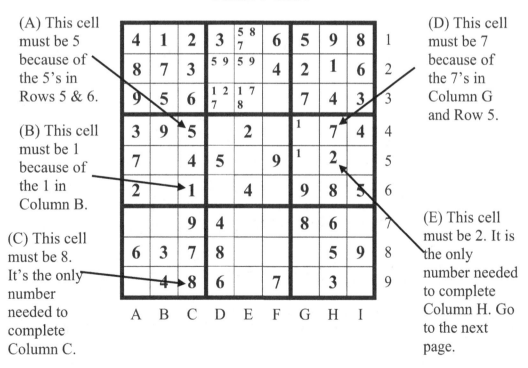

Puzzle 1 Grid 5

(A) This cell must be 5 because of the 5's in Rows 5 & 6.

(B) This cell must be 1 because of the 1 in Column B.

(C) This cell must be 8. It's the only number needed to complete Column C.

(D) This cell must be 7 because of the 7's in Column G and Row 5.

(E) This cell must be 2. It is the only number needed to complete Column H. Go to the next page.

## Grid 5

| | A | B | C | D | E | F | G | H | I | |
|---|---|---|---|---|---|---|---|---|---|---|
| 1 | 4 | 1 | 2 | 3 | 5 8 7 | 6 | 5 | 9 | 8 | 1 |
| 2 | 8 | 7 | 3 | 5 9 | 5 9 | 4 | 2 | 1 | 6 | 2 |
| 3 | 9 | 5 | 6 | 1 2 7 | 1 7 8 | | 7 | 4 | 3 | 3 |
| 4 | 3 | 9 | 5 | | 2 | | 1 | 7 | 4 | 4 |
| 5 | 7 | | 4 | 5 | | 9 | 1 | 2 | | 5 |
| 6 | 2 | | 1 | | 4 | | 9 | 8 | 5 | 6 |
| 7 | | | 9 | 4 | | | 8 | 6 | | 7 |
| 8 | 6 | 3 | 7 | 8 | | | | 5 | 9 | 8 |
| 9 | | 4 | 8 | 6 | | 7 | | 3 | | 9 |

A B C D E F G H I

## Puzzle 1 Grid 6

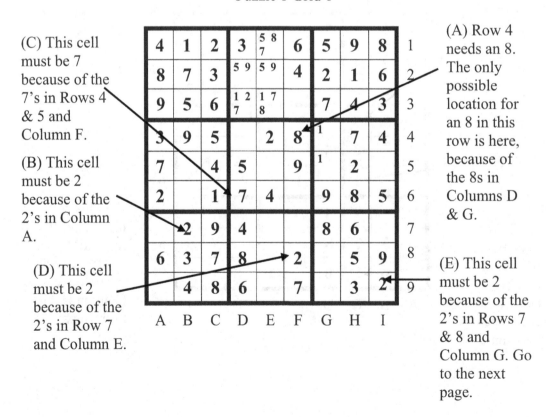

(C) This cell must be 7 because of the 7's in Rows 4 & 5 and Column F.

(B) This cell must be 2 because of the 2's in Column A.

(D) This cell must be 2 because of the 2's in Row 7 and Column E.

(A) Row 4 needs an 8. The only possible location for an 8 in this row is here, because of the 8s in Columns D & G.

(E) This cell must be 2 because of the 2's in Rows 7 & 8 and Column G. Go to the next page.

22

## Grid 6

|   | A | B | C | D | E | F | G | H | I |   |
|---|---|---|---|---|---|---|---|---|---|---|
| 1 | 4 | 1 | 2 | 3 | 5 8 7 | 6 | 5 | 9 | 8 | 1 |
| 2 | 8 | 7 | 3 | 5 9 | 5 9 | 4 | 2 | 1 | 6 | 2 |
| 3 | 9 | 5 | 6 | 1 2 7 | 1 7 8 |   | 7 | 4 | 3 | 3 |
| 4 | 3 | 9 | 5 |   | 2 | 8 | 1 | 7 | 4 | 4 |
| 5 | 7 |   | 4 | 5 |   | 9 | 1 | 2 |   | 5 |
| 6 | 2 |   | 1 | 7 | 4 |   | 9 | 8 | 5 | 6 |
| 7 |   | 2 | 9 | 4 |   |   | 8 | 6 |   | 7 |
| 8 | 6 | 3 | 7 | 8 |   | 2 |   | 5 | 9 | 8 |
| 9 |   | 4 | 8 | 6 |   | 7 |   | 3 | 2 | 9 |

A  B  C  D  E  F  G  H  I

## Puzzle 1 Grid 7

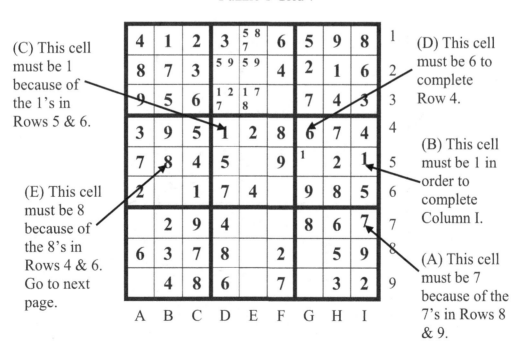

(C) This cell must be 1 because of the 1's in Rows 5 & 6.

(D) This cell must be 6 to complete Row 4.

(B) This cell must be 1 in order to complete Column I.

(E) This cell must be 8 because of the 8's in Rows 4 & 6. Go to next page.

(A) This cell must be 7 because of the 7's in Rows 8 & 9.

23

## Grid 7

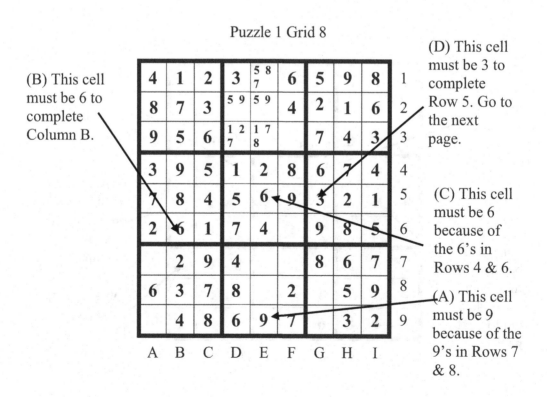

A B C D E F G H I

## Puzzle 1 Grid 8

(B) This cell must be 6 to complete Column B.

(D) This cell must be 3 to complete Row 5. Go to the next page.

(C) This cell must be 6 because of the 6's in Rows 4 & 6.

(A) This cell must be 9 because of the 9's in Rows 7 & 8.

A B C D E F G H I

24

Grid 8

| | A | B | C | D | E | F | G | H | I | |
|---|---|---|---|---|---|---|---|---|---|---|
| 1 | 4 | 1 | 2 | 3 | 5 8 7 | 6 | 5 | 9 | 8 | 1 |
| 2 | 8 | 7 | 3 | 5 9 | 5 9 | 4 | 2 | 1 | 6 | 2 |
| 3 | 9 | 5 | 6 | 1 2 7 | 1 7 8 | | 7 | 4 | 3 | 3 |
| 4 | 3 | 9 | 5 | 1 | 2 | 8 | 6 | 7 | 4 | 4 |
| 5 | 7 | 8 | 4 | 5 | 6 | 9 | 3 | 2 | 1 | 5 |
| 6 | 2 | 6 | 1 | 7 | 4 | | 9 | 8 | 5 | 6 |
| 7 | | 2 | 9 | 4 | | | 8 | 6 | 7 | 7 |
| 8 | 6 | 3 | 7 | 8 | | 2 | | 5 | 9 | 8 |
| 9 | | 4 | 8 | 6 | 9 | 7 | | 3 | 2 | 9 |

A  B  C  D  E  F  G  H  I

Puzzle 1 Grid 9

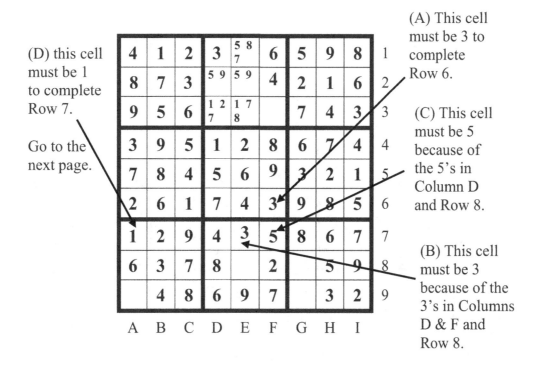

(A) This cell must be 3 to complete Row 6.

(C) This cell must be 5 because of the 5's in Column D and Row 8.

(B) This cell must be 3 because of the 3's in Columns D & F and Row 8.

(D) this cell must be 1 to complete Row 7.

Go to the next page.

## Grid 9

| | A | B | C | D | E | F | G | H | I | |
|---|---|---|---|---|---|---|---|---|---|---|
| 1 | 4 | 1 | 2 | 3 | 5 8 7 | 6 | 5 | 9 | 8 | 1 |
| 2 | 8 | 7 | 3 | 5 9 | 5 9 | 4 | 2 | 1 | 6 | 2 |
| 3 | 9 | 5 | 6 | 1 2 7 | 1 7 8 | | 7 | 4 | 3 | 3 |
| 4 | 3 | 9 | 5 | 1 | 2 | 8 | 6 | 7 | 4 | 4 |
| 5 | 7 | 8 | 4 | 5 | 6 | 9 | 3 | 2 | 1 | 5 |
| 6 | 2 | 6 | 1 | 7 | 4 | 3 | 9 | 8 | 5 | 6 |
| 7 | 1 | 2 | 9 | 4 | 3 | 5 | 8 | 6 | 7 | 7 |
| 8 | 6 | 3 | 7 | 8 | | 2 | | 5 | 9 | 8 |
| 9 | | 4 | 8 | 6 | 9 | 7 | | 3 | 2 | 9 |

A  B  C  D  E  F  G  H  I

## Puzzle 1 Grid 10

(A) This cell must be 5 to complete Column A and the lower left box.

(D) This cell must be 1 to complete Row 8 and the middle box. Go to the next page.

(C) This cell must be 4 to complete the lower right box.

(B) This cell must be 1 to complete Row 9.

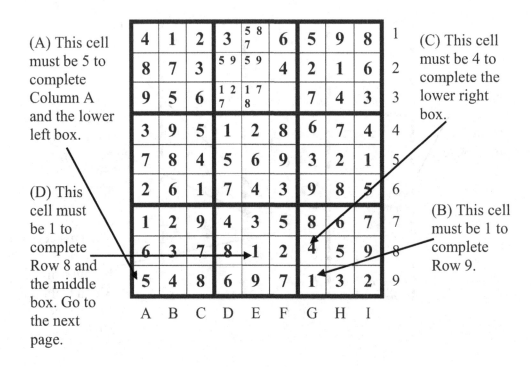

A  B  C  D  E  F  G  H  I

Grid 10

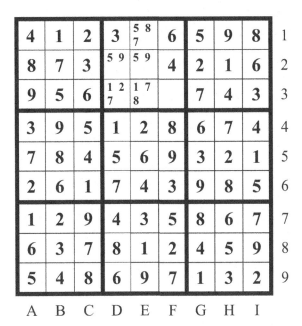

Puzzle 1 Grid 11
**Final Solution**

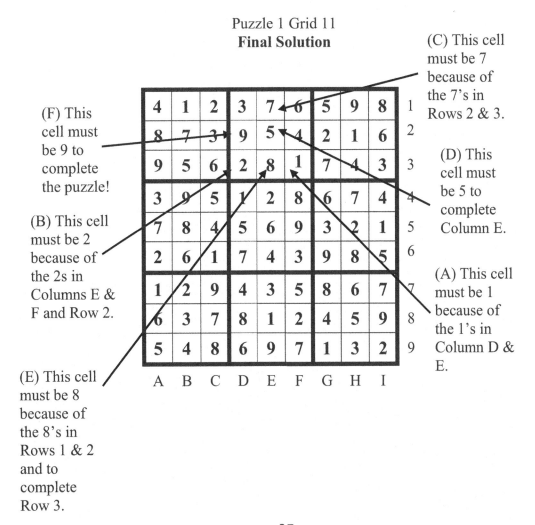

(C) This cell must be 7 because of the 7's in Rows 2 & 3.

(F) This cell must be 9 to complete the puzzle!

(D) This cell must be 5 to complete Column E.

(B) This cell must be 2 because of the 2s in Columns E & F and Row 2.

(A) This cell must be 1 because of the 1's in Column D & E.

(E) This cell must be 8 because of the 8's in Rows 1 & 2 and to complete Row 3.

27

## Worksheet for Puzzle 1A

Cut along the dotted line to remove the worksheet.

| 6 |   |   |   | 5 |   |   |   | 9 |
|---|---|---|---|---|---|---|---|---|
| 1 | 3 |   |   |   |   |   | 4 | 2 |
|   |   |   | 9 |   | 3 |   |   |   |
| 8 | 7 |   | 5 |   | 4 |   | 1 | 3 |
|   |   | 6 |   |   |   | 7 |   |   |
| 3 | 1 |   | 2 |   | 6 |   | 9 | 8 |
|   |   |   | 7 |   | 9 |   |   |   |
| 7 | 9 |   |   |   |   |   | 8 | 1 |
| 4 |   |   |   | 2 |   |   | 6 |   |

## Puzzle 1A

Puzzle 1A  Grid 1

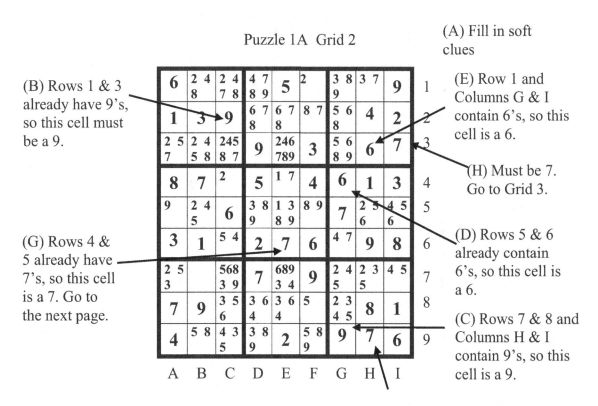

(A) Fill in soft clues

(B) Rows 1 & 3 already have 9's, so this cell must be a 9.

(E) Row 1 and Columns G & I contain 6's, so this cell is a 6.

(H) Must be 7. Go to Grid 3.

(G) Rows 4 & 5 already have 7's, so this cell is a 7. Go to the next page.

(D) Rows 5 & 6 already contain 6's, so this cell is a 6.

(C) Rows 7 & 8 and Columns H & I contain 9's, so this cell is a 9.

Puzzle 1A  Grid 2

(F) Rows 7 & 8 have 7's, so this cell must be a 7.

31

| | A | B | C | D | E | F | G | H | I | |
|---|---|---|---|---|---|---|---|---|---|---|
| | 6 | 2 4 8 | 2 4 7 8 | 4 7 8 | 5 | 2 | 3 8 3 | | 9 | 1 |
| | 1 | 3 | 9 | 6 7 8 | 6 8 | 8 7 | 5 8 | 4 | 2 | 2 |
| | 2 5 | 2 4 5 8 | 2 4 5 8 | 9 | 4 | 3 | 5 8 | 6 | 7 | 3 |
| | 8 | 7 | 2 | 5 | | 4 | 6 | 1 | 3 | 4 |
| | 9 | 2 4 5 | 6 | 3 8 | 1 3 8 9 | 8 | 7 | 2 5 | 4 5 | 5 |
| | 3 | 1 | 5 4 | 2 | 7 | 6 | 4 | | 9 8 | 6 |
| | 2 5 | | 5 8 3 | 7 | 6 8 3 4 | 9 | 2 4 5 | 2 3 5 | 4 5 | 7 |
| | 7 | 9 | 3 5 | 3 6 4 | 3 6 4 | 5 | 2 3 4 5 | 8 | 1 | 8 |
| | 4 | 5 8 | 3 5 | 3 8 | 2 | 5 8 | 9 | 7 | 6 | 9 |

Puzzle 1A  Grid 3

(A) The cell must be 7 because Columns A & B and Row 3 already have 7's.

(B) Columns B & C already have 9's, so this cell is a 9.

(F) Only number missing in this row is 2.

(G) Must be 2.

(C) Columns A & C and Row 9 have 6's, so this cell is a 6.

(E) Must be 2.

(D) Rows 5 & 6 have 9's, so this cell is a 9. Go to the next page.

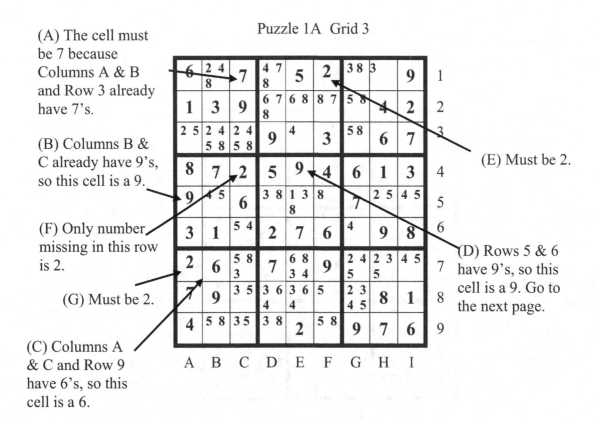

Grid 3

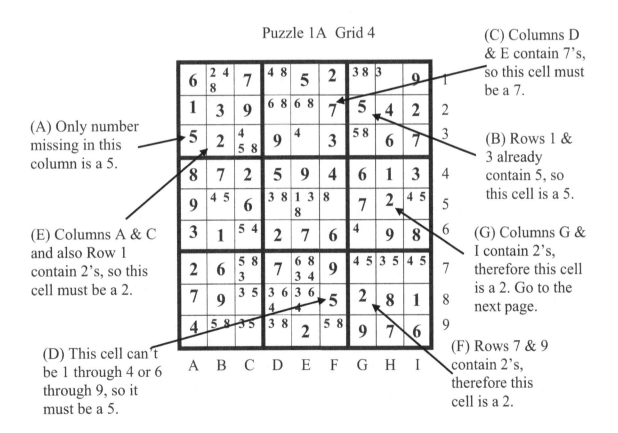

Puzzle 1A  Grid 4

(A) Only number missing in this column is a 5.

(E) Columns A & C and also Row 1 contain 2's, so this cell must be a 2.

(D) This cell can't be 1 through 4 or 6 through 9, so it must be a 5.

(C) Columns D & E contain 7's, so this cell must be a 7.

(B) Rows 1 & 3 already contain 5, so this cell is a 5.

(G) Columns G & I contain 2's, therefore this cell is a 2. Go to the next page.

(F) Rows 7 & 9 contain 2's, therefore this cell is a 2.

Grid 4

Puzzle 1A  Grid 5

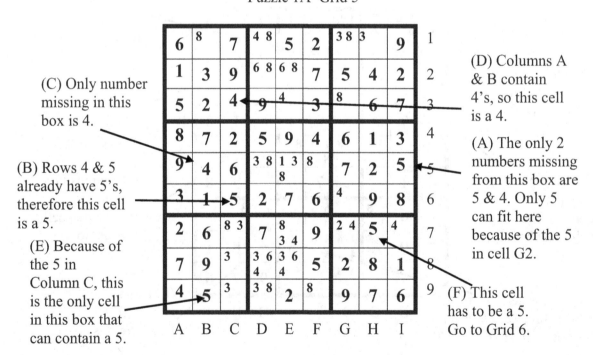

(C) Only number missing in this box is 4.

(B) Rows 4 & 5 already have 5's, therefore this cell is a 5.

(E) Because of the 5 in Column C, this is the only cell in this box that can contain a 5.

(D) Columns A & B contain 4's, so this cell is a 4.

(A) The only 2 numbers missing from this box are 5 & 4. Only 5 can fit here because of the 5 in cell G2.

(F) This cell has to be a 5. Go to Grid 6.

34

## Grid 5

| | A | B | C | D | E | F | G | H | I | |
|---|---|---|---|---|---|---|---|---|---|---|
| 1 | 6 | (8) | 7 | (4 8) | 5 | 2 | (3 8) | (3) | 9 | 1 |
| 2 | 1 | 3 | 9 | (6 8) | (6 8) | 7 | 5 | 4 | 2 | 2 |
| 3 | 5 | 2 | 4 | 9 | (4) | 3 | (8) | 6 | 7 | 3 |
| 4 | 8 | 7 | 2 | 5 | 9 | 4 | 6 | 1 | 3 | 4 |
| 5 | 9 | 4 | 6 | (3 8) | (1 3 8) | 8 | 7 | 2 | 5 | 5 |
| 6 | 3 | 1 | 5 | 2 | 7 | 6 | (4) | 9 | 8 | 6 |
| 7 | 2 | 6 | (8 3) | 7 | (8 3 4) | 9 | (4) | 5 | (4) | 7 |
| 8 | 7 | 9 | (3) | (3 6 4) | (3 6 4) | 5 | 2 | 8 | 1 | 8 |
| 9 | 4 | 5 | (3) | (3 8) | 2 | (8) | 9 | 7 | 6 | 9 |
| | A | B | C | D | E | F | G | H | I | |

## Puzzle 1A  Grid 6

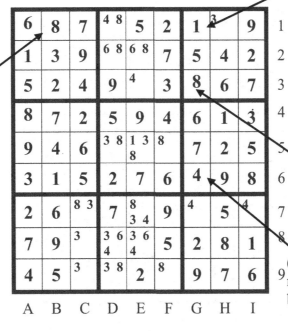

(A) The only number missing from this column is 8.

(B) The only number missing from this box is a 4.

(C) The only numbers missing from Column G are 3 & 8 – 8 can only go here.

(D) Columns H & I contain 1's, so this cell is a 1. Go to the next page.

Grid 6

| | A | B | C | D | E | F | G | H | I | |
|---|---|---|---|---|---|---|---|---|---|---|
| | 6 | 8 | 7 | ⁴ | 5 | 2 | 1 | ³ | 9 | 1 |
| | 1 | 3 | 9 | 6 8 / 6 8 | | 7 | 5 | 4 | 2 | 2 |
| | 5 | 2 | 4 | 9 | | 3 | 8 | 6 | 7 | 3 |
| | 8 | 7 | 2 | 5 | 9 | 4 | 6 | 1 | 3 | 4 |
| | 9 | 4 | 6 | 3 8 / 1 3 8 | 8 | | 7 | 2 | 5 | 5 |
| | 3 | 1 | 5 | 2 | 7 | 6 | 4 | 9 | 8 | 6 |
| | 2 | 6 | 8 3 | 7 | 8 / 3 4 | 9 | | 5 | ⁴ | 7 |
| | 7 | 9 | 3 | 3 6 4 / 3 6 4 | | 5 | 2 | 8 | 1 | 8 |
| | 4 | 5 | 3 | 3 8 | 2 | ⁸ | 9 | 7 | 6 | 9 |

Puzzle 1A  Grid 7

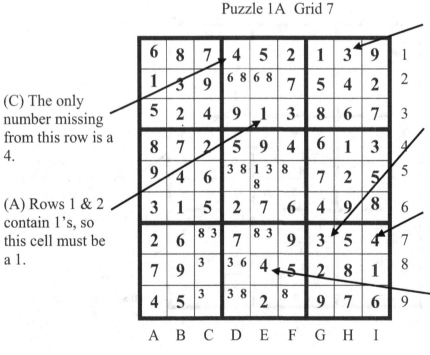

(B) The only number missing from this column is 3.

(C) The only number missing from this row is a 4.

(D) Columns H & I already have 3's, so this cell must be a 3.

(A) Rows 1 & 2 contain 1's, so this cell must be a 1.

(E) The only number missing from this box is a 4.

(F) Rows 7 & 9 and Columns D & F contain 4's, so this cell must be a 4. Go to the next page.

36

## Grid 7

| | A | B | C | D | E | F | G | H | I | |
|---|---|---|---|---|---|---|---|---|---|---|
| | 6 | 8 | 7 | 4 | 5 | 2 | 1 | 3 | 9 | 1 |
| | 1 | 3 | 9 | 6 8 / 6 8 | | 7 | 5 | 4 | 2 | 2 |
| | 5 | 2 | 4 | 9 | 1 | 3 | 8 | 6 | 7 | 3 |
| | 8 | 7 | 2 | 5 | 9 | 4 | 6 | 1 | 3 | 4 |
| | 9 | 4 | 6 | 3 8 / 3 8 | 8 | | 7 | 2 | 5 | 5 |
| | 3 | 1 | 5 | 2 | 7 | 6 | 4 | 9 | 8 | 6 |
| | 2 | 6 | 8 | 7 | 8 | 9 | 3 | 5 | 4 | 7 |
| | 7 | 9 | 3 | 3 6 | 4 | 5 | 2 | 8 | 1 | 8 |
| | 4 | 5 | 3 | 3 8 | 2 | 8 | 9 | 7 | 6 | 9 |

A   B   C   D   E   F   G   H   I

## Puzzle 1A  Grid 8

(C) The only number missing from this box is an 8.

(B) Columns D & F contain 6's, therefore this cell is a 6.

(D) Because Rows 4 & 6 contain 1's, this cell is a 1.

(G) The only number missing from Row 8 is a 3.

(F) Must be 1. Go to the next page.

(E) Must be 3.

(A) Must be 6.

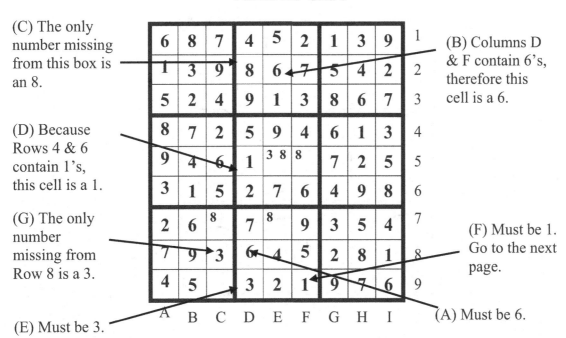

37

## Grid 8

| | A | B | C | D | E | F | G | H | I | |
|---|---|---|---|---|---|---|---|---|---|---|
| | 6 | 8 | 7 | 4 | 5 | 2 | 1 | 3 | 9 | 1 |
| | 1 | 3 | 9 | 8 | 6 | 7 | 5 | 4 | 2 | 2 |
| | 5 | 2 | 4 | 9 | 1 | 3 | 8 | 6 | 7 | 3 |
| | 8 | 7 | 2 | 5 | 9 | 4 | 6 | 1 | 3 | 4 |
| | 9 | 4 | 6 | 1 | 3 8 | 8 | 7 | 2 | 5 | 5 |
| | 3 | 1 | 5 | 2 | 7 | 6 | 4 | 9 | 8 | 6 |
| | 2 | 6 | 8 | 7 | 8 | 9 | 3 | 5 | 4 | 7 |
| | 7 | 9 | 3 | 6 | 4 | 5 | 2 | 8 | 1 | 8 |
| | 4 | 5 | | 3 | 2 | 1 | 9 | 7 | 6 | 9 |

## Puzzle 1A  Grid 9
### Final Solution

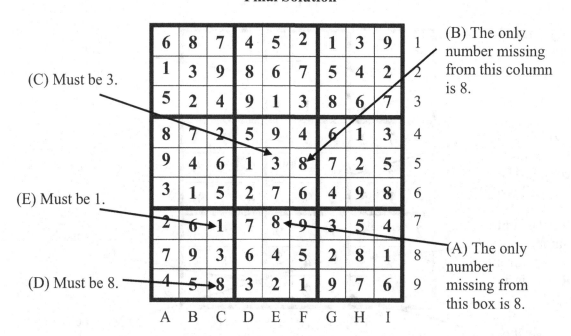

(B) The only number missing from this column is 8.

(C) Must be 3.

(E) Must be 1.

(D) Must be 8.

(A) The only number missing from this box is 8.

| | A | B | C | D | E | F | G | H | I | |
|---|---|---|---|---|---|---|---|---|---|---|
| | 6 | 8 | 7 | 4 | 5 | 2 | 1 | 3 | 9 | 1 |
| | 1 | 3 | 9 | 8 | 6 | 7 | 5 | 4 | 2 | 2 |
| | 5 | 2 | 4 | 9 | 1 | 3 | 8 | 6 | 7 | 3 |
| | 8 | 7 | 2 | 5 | 9 | 4 | 6 | 1 | 3 | 4 |
| | 9 | 4 | 6 | 1 | 3 | 8 | 7 | 2 | 5 | 5 |
| | 3 | 1 | 5 | 2 | 7 | 6 | 4 | 9 | 8 | 6 |
| | 2 | 6 | 1 | 7 | 8 | 9 | 3 | 5 | 4 | 7 |
| | 7 | 9 | 3 | 6 | 4 | 5 | 2 | 8 | 1 | 8 |
| | 4 | 5 | 8 | 3 | 2 | 1 | 9 | 7 | 6 | 9 |

38

## Worksheet for Puzzle 2

Cut along the dotted line to remove the worksheet.

| | | 5 | | | 6 | | 7 | |
|---|---|---|---|---|---|---|---|---|
| 7 | | | 9 | 5 | | 4 | | |
| | 1 | 9 | | | 4 | 2 | | 3 |
| 3 | | 4 | 2 | | 9 | | 8 | |
| | 9 | | | 3 | | | 6 | |
| | 8 | | 7 | | 5 | 3 | | 2 |
| 9 | | 3 | 5 | | | 6 | 4 | |
| | | 1 | | 2 | 7 | | | 9 |
| | 5 | | 6 | | | 8 | | |

## Puzzle 2

This is another fairly simple puzzle. Proceed with steps A – G, referring back to the previous grid to help understand the solving process. Work the process step by step to reach the solution.

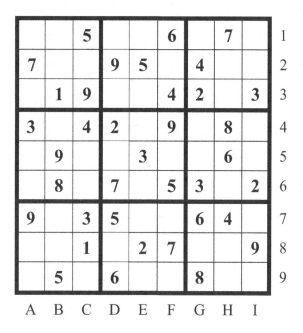

Puzzle 2 Grid 1

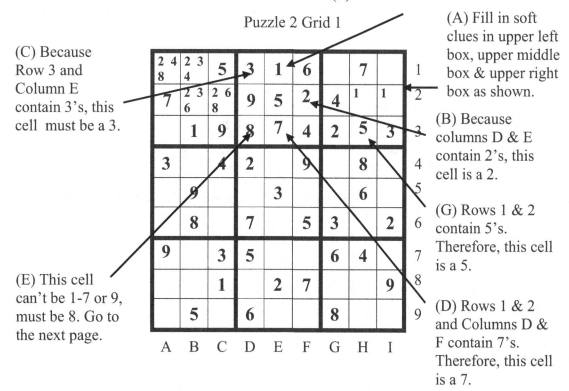

(F) This cell has to be a 1.

(A) Fill in soft clues in upper left box, upper middle box & upper right box as shown.

(C) Because Row 3 and Column E contain 3's, this cell must be a 3.

(B) Because columns D & E contain 2's, this cell is a 2.

(G) Rows 1 & 2 contain 5's. Therefore, this cell is a 5.

(E) This cell can't be 1-7 or 9, must be 8. Go to the next page.

(D) Rows 1 & 2 and Columns D & F contain 7's. Therefore, this cell is a 7.

41

| | A | B | C | D | E | F | G | H | I | |
|---|---|---|---|---|---|---|---|---|---|---|
| 1 | 2 4 8 | 2 3 4 | 5 | 3 | 1 | 6 | | 7 | | 1 |
| 2 | 7 | 2 3 6 | 2 6 8 | 9 | 5 | 2 | 4 | 1 | 1 | 2 |
| 3 | | 1 | 9 | 8 | 7 | 4 | 2 | 5 | 3 | 3 |
| 4 | 3 | | 4 | 2 | | 9 | | 8 | | 4 |
| 5 | | 9 | | | 3 | | | 6 | | 5 |
| 6 | | 8 | | 7 | | 5 | 3 | | 2 | 6 |
| 7 | 9 | | 3 | 5 | | | 6 | 4 | | 7 |
| 8 | | | 1 | | 2 | 7 | | | 9 | 8 |
| 9 | | 5 | | 6 | | | 8 | | | 9 |

A  B  C  D  E  F  G  H  I

With the upper middle box completed, now work on the upper right box.

Puzzle 2  Grid 2

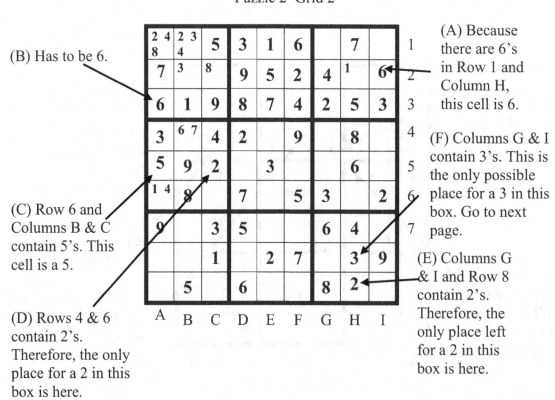

(B) Has to be 6.

(A) Because there are 6's in Row 1 and Column H, this cell is 6.

(F) Columns G & I contain 3's. This is the only possible place for a 3 in this box. Go to next page.

(C) Row 6 and Columns B & C contain 5's. This cell is a 5.

(E) Columns G & I and Row 8 contain 2's. Therefore, the only place left for a 2 in this box is here.

(D) Rows 4 & 6 contain 2's. Therefore, the only place for a 2 in this box is here.

## Grid 2

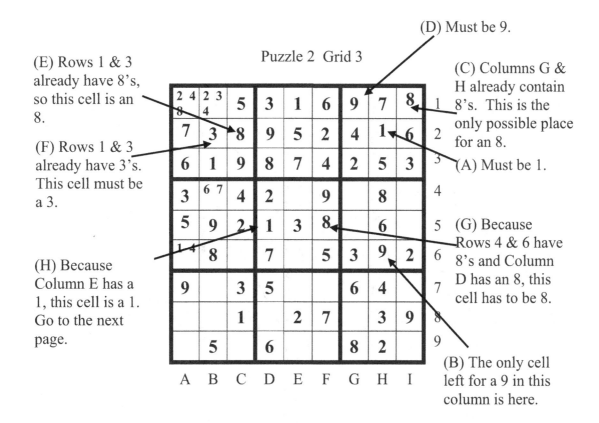

Grid 2 (top grid):

|   | A | B | C | D | E | F | G | H | I |   |
|---|---|---|---|---|---|---|---|---|---|---|
| 1 | 2 4 8 | 2 3 4 | 5 | 3 | 1 | 6 |   | 7 |   | 1 |
| 2 | 7 | 3 | 8 | 9 | 5 | 2 | 4 | 1 | 6 | 2 |
| 3 | 6 | 1 | 9 | 8 | 7 | 4 | 2 | 5 | 3 | 3 |
| 4 | 3 | 6 7 | 4 | 2 |   | 9 |   | 8 |   | 4 |
| 5 | 5 | 9 | 2 |   | 3 |   |   | 6 |   | 5 |
| 6 | 1 4 | 8 |   | 7 |   | 5 | 3 |   | 2 | 6 |
| 7 | 9 |   | 3 | 5 |   |   | 6 | 4 |   | 7 |
| 8 |   |   | 1 |   | 2 | 7 |   | 3 | 9 | 8 |
| 9 |   | 5 |   | 6 |   |   | 8 | 2 |   | 9 |

A  B  C  D  E  F  G  H  I

---

Puzzle 2  Grid 3

(E) Rows 1 & 3 already have 8's, so this cell is an 8.

(F) Rows 1 & 3 already have 3's. This cell must be a 3.

(H) Because Column E has a 1, this cell is a 1. Go to the next page.

(D) Must be 9.

(C) Columns G & H already contain 8's. This is the only possible place for an 8.

(A) Must be 1.

(G) Because Rows 4 & 6 have 8's and Column D has an 8, this cell has to be 8.

(B) The only cell left for a 9 in this column is here.

Grid 3 (bottom grid):

|   | A | B | C | D | E | F | G | H | I |   |
|---|---|---|---|---|---|---|---|---|---|---|
| 1 | 2 4 8 | 2 3 4 | 5 | 3 | 1 | 6 | 9 | 7 | 8 | 1 |
| 2 | 7 | 3 | 8 | 9 | 5 | 2 | 4 | 1 | 6 | 2 |
| 3 | 6 | 1 | 9 | 8 | 7 | 4 | 2 | 5 | 3 | 3 |
| 4 | 3 | 6 7 | 4 | 2 |   | 9 |   | 8 |   | 4 |
| 5 | 5 | 9 | 2 | 1 | 3 | 8 |   | 6 |   | 5 |
| 6 | 1 4 | 8 |   | 7 |   | 5 | 3 | 9 | 2 | 6 |
| 7 | 9 |   | 3 | 5 |   |   | 6 | 4 |   | 7 |
| 8 |   |   | 1 |   | 2 | 7 |   | 3 | 9 | 8 |
| 9 |   | 5 |   | 6 |   |   | 8 | 2 |   | 9 |

A  B  C  D  E  F  G  H  I

Grid 3

| | | | | | | | | | |
|---|---|---|---|---|---|---|---|---|---|
| ²⁴₈ | ²³₄ | 5 | 3 | 1 | 6 | 9 | 7 | 8 | 1 |
| 7 | 3 | 8 | 9 | 5 | 2 | 4 | 1 | 6 | 2 |
| 6 | 1 | 9 | 8 | 7 | 4 | 2 | 5 | 3 | 3 |
| 3 | ⁶⁷ | 4 | 2 | | 9 | | 8 | | 4 |
| 5 | 9 | 2 | 1 | 3 | 8 | | 6 | | 5 |
| ¹⁴ | 8 | | 7 | | 5 | 3 | 9 | 2 | 6 |
| 9 | | 3 | 5 | | | 6 | 4 | | 7 |
| | | 1 | | 2 | 7 | | 3 | 9 | 8 |
| | 5 | | 6 | | | 8 | 2 | | 9 |

A  B  C  D  E  F  G  H  I

Puzzle 2  Grid 4

(A) Because Column F and Row 4 contain 4's, this cell is a 4.

(G) The only number missing from this row is a 1. Go to the next page.

(F) Because Rows 4 & 5 and Column A contain a 6, this cell is a 6.

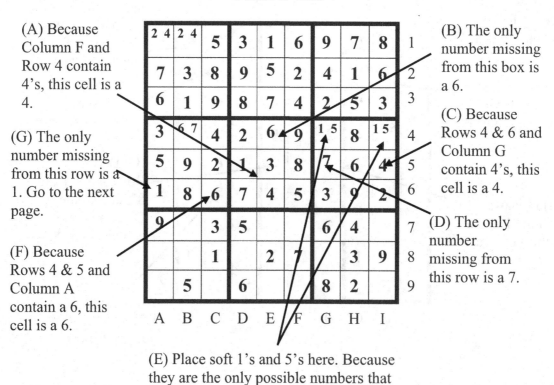

(B) The only number missing from this box is a 6.

(C) Because Rows 4 & 6 and Column G contain 4's, this cell is a 4.

(D) The only number missing from this row is a 7.

(E) Place soft 1's and 5's here. Because they are the only possible numbers that can be place in these cells.

44

Grid 4

| | | | | | | | | | |
|---|---|---|---|---|---|---|---|---|---|
| 2 4 | 2 4 | 5 | 3 | 1 | 6 | 9 | 7 | 8 | 1 |
| 7 | 3 | 8 | 9 | 5 | 2 | 4 | 1 | 6 | 2 |
| 6 | 1 | 9 | 8 | 7 | 4 | 2 | 5 | 3 | 3 |
| 3 | 6 7 | 4 | 2 | 6 | 9 | 1 5 | 8 | 1 5 | 4 |
| 5 | 9 | 2 | 1 | 3 | 8 | 7 | 6 | 4 | 5 |
| 1 | 8 | 6 | 7 | 4 | 5 | 3 | 9 | 2 | 6 |
| 9 | | 3 | 5 | | | 6 | 4 | | 7 |
| | | 1 | | 2 | 7 | | 3 | 9 | 8 |
| | 5 | | 6 | | | 8 | 2 | | 9 |

A  B  C  D  E  F  G  H  I

Puzzle 2  Grid 5

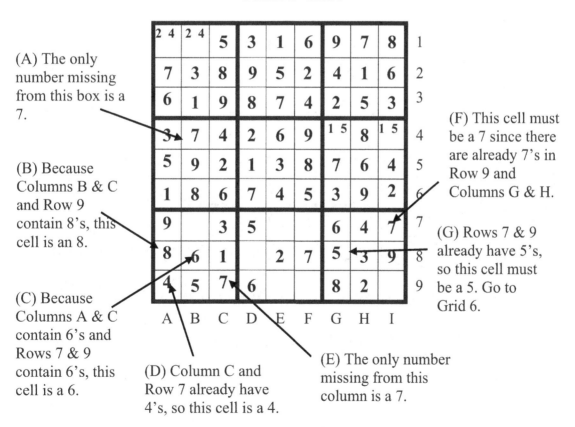

(A) The only number missing from this box is a 7.

(B) Because Columns B & C and Row 9 contain 8's, this cell is an 8.

(C) Because Columns A & C contain 6's and Rows 7 & 9 contain 6's, this cell is a 6.

(D) Column C and Row 7 already have 4's, so this cell is a 4.

(E) The only number missing from this column is a 7.

(F) This cell must be a 7 since there are already 7's in Row 9 and Columns G & H.

(G) Rows 7 & 9 already have 5's, so this cell must be a 5. Go to Grid 6.

45

## Grid 5

| | A | B | C | D | E | F | G | H | I | |
|---|---|---|---|---|---|---|---|---|---|---|
| 1 | 2 4 | 2 4 | 5 | 3 | 1 | 6 | 9 | 7 | 8 | 1 |
| 2 | 7 | 3 | 8 | 9 | 5 | 2 | 4 | 1 | 6 | 2 |
| 3 | 6 | 1 | 9 | 8 | 7 | 4 | 2 | 5 | 3 | 3 |
| 4 | 3 | 7 | 4 | 2 | 6 | 9 | 1 5 | 8 | 1 5 | 4 |
| 5 | 5 | 9 | 2 | 1 | 3 | 8 | 7 | 6 | 4 | 5 |
| 6 | 1 | 8 | 6 | 7 | 4 | 5 | 3 | 9 | 2 | 6 |
| 7 | 9 | | 3 | 5 | | | 6 | 4 | 7 | 7 |
| 8 | 8 | 6 | 1 | | 2 | 7 | 5 | 3 | 9 | 8 |
| 9 | 4 | 5 | 7 | 6 | | | 8 | 2 | | 9 |

A  B  C  D  E  F  G  H  I

(G) The only number missing from this row is a 4. Go to Grid 7.

## Puzzle 2  Grid 6

(F) The only number missing here is a 2.

(B) The only number missing from the lower left box is a 2.

(D) The only number missing from this row is a 4.

| | A | B | C | D | E | F | G | H | I | |
|---|---|---|---|---|---|---|---|---|---|---|
| 1 | 2 | 4 | 5 | 3 | 1 | 6 | 9 | 7 | 8 | 1 |
| 2 | 7 | 3 | 8 | 9 | 5 | 2 | 4 | 1 | 6 | 2 |
| 3 | 6 | 1 | 9 | 8 | 7 | 4 | 2 | 5 | 3 | 3 |
| 4 | 3 | 7 | 4 | 2 | 6 | 9 | 1 5 | 8 | 1 5 | 4 |
| 5 | 5 | 9 | 2 | 1 | 3 | 8 | 7 | 6 | 4 | 5 |
| 6 | 1 | 8 | 6 | 7 | 4 | 5 | 3 | 9 | 2 | 6 |
| 7 | 9 | 2 | 3 | 5 | 8 | 1 | 6 | 4 | 7 | 7 |
| 8 | 8 | 6 | 1 | 4 | 2 | 7 | 5 | 3 | 9 | 8 |
| 9 | 4 | 5 | 7 | 6 | 9 | 3 | 8 | 2 | 1 | 9 |

A  B  C  D  E  F  G  H  I

(E) This is the only possible cell for 1.

(A) The only number missing from the lower right box is a 1.

(C) Rows 7 & 8 and Column E contain 3's, so this cell must be a 3.

(H) Must be 8.

(I) Must be 9.

46

Grid 6

| 2 | 4 | 5 | 3 | 1 | 6 | 9 | 7 | 8 | 1 |
| 7 | 3 | 8 | 9 | 5 | 2 | 4 | 1 | 6 | 2 |
| 6 | 1 | 9 | 8 | 7 | 4 | 2 | 5 | 3 | 3 |
| 3 | 7 | 4 | 2 | 6 | 9 | 1 5 | 8 | 1 5 | 4 |
| 5 | 9 | 2 | 1 | 3 | 8 | 7 | 6 | 4 | 5 |
| 1 | 8 | 6 | 7 | 4 | 5 | 3 | 9 | 2 | 6 |
| 9 | 2 | 3 | 5 | 8 | 1 | 6 | 4 | 7 | 7 |
| 8 | 6 | 1 | 4 | 2 | 7 | 5 | 3 | 9 | 8 |
| 4 | 5 | 7 | 6 | 9 | 3 | 8 | 2 | 1 | 9 |

A  B  C  D  E  F  G  H  I

Puzzle 2  Grid 7
**Final Solution**

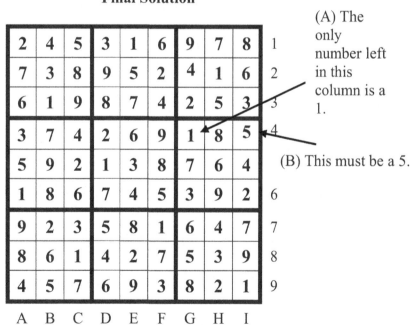

(A) The only number left in this column is a 1.

(B) This must be a 5.

## Worksheet for Puzzle 2A

Cut along the dotted line to remove the worksheet.

| 6 |   |   |   |   |   | 9 |   |   |
|---|---|---|---|---|---|---|---|---|
|   |   |   | 9 | 6 |   |   | 8 |   |
| 1 |   | 5 |   | 8 |   |   |   | 3 |
|   |   |   |   |   | 1 | 3 | 4 | 8 |
| 9 |   |   |   |   |   |   |   | 7 |
| 8 | 4 | 2 | 6 |   |   |   |   |   |
| 3 |   |   |   | 5 |   | 2 |   | 1 |
|   | 2 |   |   | 7 | 9 |   |   |   |
|   |   | 7 |   |   |   |   |   | 5 |

## Puzzle 2A

Puzzle 2A  Grid 1

|   | A | B | C | D | E | F | G | H | I |   |
|---|---|---|---|---|---|---|---|---|---|---|
| 1 | 6 |   |   |   |   |   | 9 |   |   |   |
| 2 |   |   |   | 9 | 6 |   |   | 8 |   |   |
| 3 | 1 |   | 5 |   | 8 |   |   |   | 3 |   |
| 4 |   |   |   |   |   | 1 | 3 | 4 | 8 |   |
| 5 | 9 |   |   |   |   |   |   |   | 7 |   |
| 6 | 8 | 4 | 2 | 6 |   |   |   |   |   |   |
| 7 | 3 |   |   |   | 5 |   | 2 |   | 1 |   |
| 8 |   | 2 |   |   | 7 | 9 |   |   |   |   |
| 9 |   |   | 7 |   |   |   |   |   | 5 |   |

A  B  C  D  E  F  G  H  I

Puzzle 2A  Grid 2

(A) Fill in soft clues as shown.

(F) Cell must be 2 because of 2's in Columns B & C.

(G) The only place remaining in Column I for a 2 is here.

(E) Cell must be 6.

(H) Can't be 1 through 3, can't be 5 through 9, so it must be 4. Go to the next page.

(D) Can't be 1-4 or 6-9, must be 5.

(C) Cell D6 contains a 6, therefore the only place remaining in Column I for a 6 is here.

(B) Can't be 1 through 3 and can't be 5 through 9, so this cell must be 4.

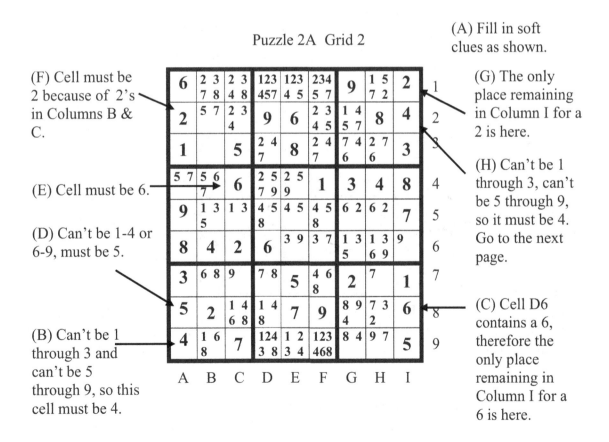

Grid 2

Puzzle 2A  Grid 3

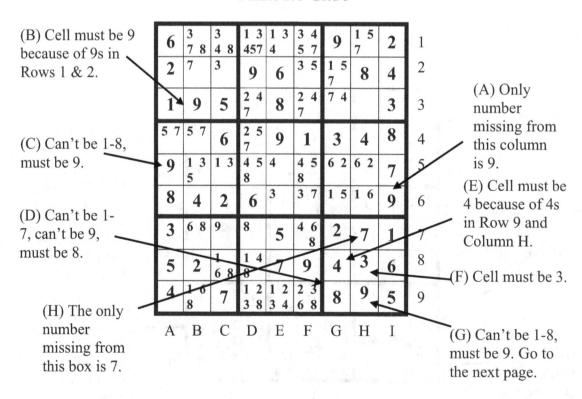

(B) Cell must be 9 because of 9s in Rows 1 & 2.

(C) Can't be 1-8, must be 9.

(D) Can't be 1-7, can't be 9, must be 8.

(H) The only number missing from this box is 7.

(A) Only number missing from this column is 9.

(E) Cell must be 4 because of 4s in Row 9 and Column H.

(F) Cell must be 3.

(G) Can't be 1-8, must be 9. Go to the next page.

## Grid 3

| | A | B | C | D | E | F | G | H | I |
|---|---|---|---|---|---|---|---|---|---|
| 1 | 6 | 3 7 8 | 3 4 8 | 1 3 457 | 1 3 4 | 3 4 5 7 | 9 | 1 5 7 | 2 |
| 2 | 2 | 7 | 3 | 9 | 6 | 3 5 | 1 5 7 | 8 | 4 |
| 3 | 1 | 9 | 5 | 2 4 7 | 8 | 2 4 7 | 7 | | 3 |
| 4 | 5 7 | 5 7 | 6 | 2 5 7 | 9 | 1 | 3 | 4 | 8 |
| 5 | 9 | 1 3 5 | 1 3 | 4 5 8 | 4 | 4 5 8 | 6 2 | 2 | 7 |
| 6 | 8 | 4 | 2 | 6 | 3 | 3 7 | 1 5 | 1 | 9 |
| 7 | 3 | 6 8 9 | | 8 | 5 | 4 6 8 | 2 | 7 | 1 |
| 8 | 5 | 2 | 1 6 8 | 1 8 | 7 | 9 | 4 | 3 | 6 |
| 9 | 4 | 1 6 | 7 | 1 2 3 | 1 2 3 4 | 2 3 6 | 8 | 9 | 5 |

## Puzzle 2A  Grid 4

(F) Cell must be 4.

(E) Can't be 1 through 6 or 8 & 9, so this cell must be 7.

(D) Can't be 1 or 2, can't be 4 through 9, so this cell must be 3.

(A) Cell must be 7.

(B) Can't be 1 through 4, can't be 6 through 9, so this cell must be 5.

(C) Only number missing from this row is 2.

(G) Must be 7.

(H) Has to be 6.

(I) Has to be 7. Go to the next page.

| | A | B | C | D | E | F | G | H | I |
|---|---|---|---|---|---|---|---|---|---|
| 1 | 6 | 8 | 4 | 1 3 457 | 1 3 4 | 3 4 5 7 | 9 | 1 5 | 2 |
| 2 | 2 | 7 | 3 | 9 | 6 | 3 5 | 1 5 | 8 | 4 |
| 3 | 1 | 9 | 5 | 2 4 7 | 8 | 2 4 7 | 7 | 6 | 3 |
| 4 | 7 | 5 | 6 | 2 | 9 | 1 | 3 | 4 | 8 |
| 5 | 9 | 1 3 | 1 3 | 4 5 8 | 4 | 4 5 8 | 6 2 2 | | 7 |
| 6 | 8 | 4 | 2 | 6 | 3 | 7 | 1 5 1 | | 9 |
| 7 | 3 | 6 8 9 | | 8 | 5 | 4 6 8 | 2 | 7 | 1 |
| 8 | 5 | 2 | 1 6 8 | 1 8 | 7 | 9 | 4 | 3 | 6 |
| 9 | 4 | 1 6 | 7 | 1 2 3 | 1 2 3 4 | 2 3 6 | 8 | 9 | 5 |

## Grid 4

|   | A | B | C | D | E | F | G | H | I |
|---|---|---|---|---|---|---|---|---|---|
| 1 | 6 | (8) | 4 | (1 3 5 7) | (1 3 4) | (3 5 7) | 9 | (1 5) | 2 |
| 2 | 2 | 7 | 3 | 9 | 6 | (5) | (1 5) | 8 | 4 |
| 3 | 1 | 9 | 5 | (2 4) | 8 | (2 4) | 7 | 6 | 3 |
| 4 | 7 | 5 | 6 | 2 | 9 | 1 | 3 | 4 | 8 |
| 5 | 9 | (1 3) | (1 3) | (4 5 8) | 4 | (4 5 8) | (6 2) | (2) | 7 |
| 6 | 8 | 4 | 2 | 6 | (3) | 7 | (1 5) | (1) | 9 |
| 7 | 3 | (6 8) | 9 | 8 | 5 | (4 6 8) | 2 | 7 | 1 |
| 8 | 5 | 2 | (1 8) | (1 8) | 7 | 9 | 4 | 3 | 6 |
| 9 | 4 | (1 6) | 7 | (1 2 3) | (1 2 3) | (2 3 6) | 8 | 9 | 5 |

## Puzzle 2A   Grid 5

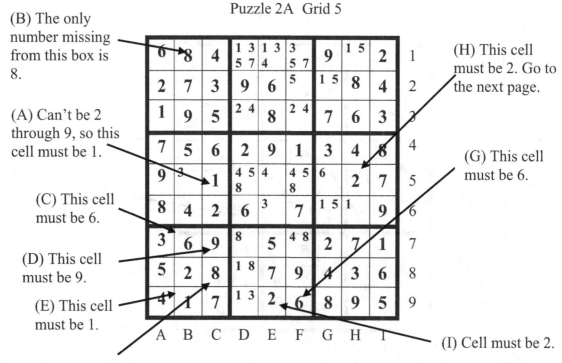

(B) The only number missing from this box is 8.

(A) Can't be 2 through 9, so this cell must be 1.

(C) This cell must be 6.

(D) This cell must be 9.

(E) This cell must be 1.

(F) Only number missing in this box is 8.

(H) This cell must be 2. Go to the next page.

(G) This cell must be 6.

(I) Cell must be 2.

## Grid 5

| | A | B | C | D | E | F | G | H | I | |
|---|---|---|---|---|---|---|---|---|---|---|
| 1 | 6 | 8 | 4 | 1 3 5 7 | 1 3 | 3 5 | 9 | 1 5 | 2 | 1 |
| 2 | 2 | 7 | 3 | 9 | 6 | 5 | 1 5 | 8 | 4 | 2 |
| 3 | 1 | 9 | 5 | 2 4 | 8 | 2 4 | 7 | 6 | 3 | 3 |
| 4 | 7 | 5 | 6 | 2 | 9 | 1 | 3 | 4 | 8 | 4 |
| 5 | 9 | 3 | 1 | 4 5 8 | 4 | 4 5 8 | 6 | 2 | 7 | 5 |
| 6 | 8 | 4 | 2 | 6 | 3 | 7 | 1 5 | 1 | 9 | 6 |
| 7 | 3 | 6 | 9 | 8 | 5 | 4 8 | 2 | 7 | 1 | 7 |
| 8 | 5 | 2 | 8 | 1 | 7 | 9 | 4 | 3 | 6 | 8 |
| 9 | 4 | 1 | 7 | 3 | 2 | 6 | 8 | 9 | 5 | 9 |

A B C D E F G H I

## Puzzle 2A  Grid 6

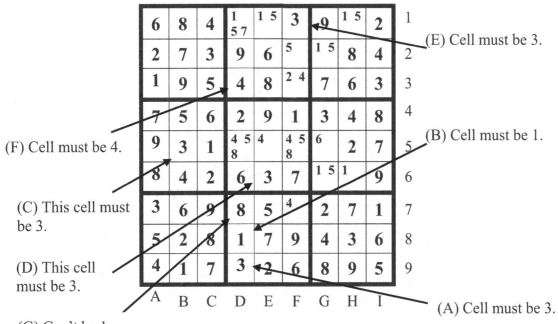

(E) Cell must be 3.

(F) Cell must be 4.

(B) Cell must be 1.

(C) This cell must be 3.

(D) This cell must be 3.

(A) Cell must be 3.

(G) Can't be 1 through 7 or 9, so this cell must be 8. Go to the next page.

## Grid 6

| | A | B | C | D | E | F | G | H | I | |
|---|---|---|---|---|---|---|---|---|---|---|
| | 6 | 8 | 4 | 1 5 7 | 1 | 3 | 9 | 1 5 | 2 | 1 |
| | 2 | 7 | 3 | 9 | 6 | 5 | 1 5 | 8 | 4 | 2 |
| | 1 | 9 | 5 | 4 | 8 | 2 | 7 | 6 | 3 | 3 |
| | 7 | 5 | 6 | 2 | 9 | 1 | 3 | 4 | 8 | 4 |
| | 9 | 3 | 1 | 4 5 | 4 | 4 5 8 | 6 | 2 | 7 | 5 |
| | 8 | 4 | 2 | 6 | 3 | 7 | 1 5 | 1 | 9 | 6 |
| | 3 | 6 | 9 | 8 | 5 | 4 | 2 | 7 | 1 | 7 |
| | 5 | 2 | 8 | 1 | 7 | 9 | 4 | 3 | 6 | 8 |
| | 4 | 1 | 7 | 3 | 2 | 6 | 8 | 9 | 5 | 9 |

A B C D E F G H I

## Puzzle 2A  Grid 7

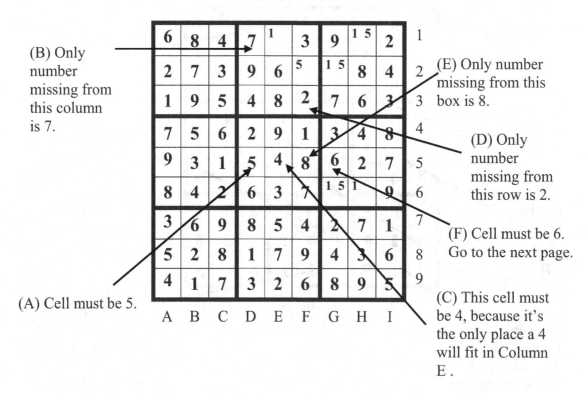

(B) Only number missing from this column is 7.

(E) Only number missing from this box is 8.

(D) Only number missing from this row is 2.

(F) Cell must be 6. Go to the next page.

(A) Cell must be 5.

(C) This cell must be 4, because it's the only place a 4 will fit in Column E.

Grid 7

| | A | B | C | D | E | F | G | H | I | |
|---|---|---|---|---|---|---|---|---|---|---|
| 1 | 6 | 8 | 4 | 7 ¹ | | 3 | 9 | ¹ ⁵ | 2 | 1 |
| 2 | 2 | 7 | 3 | 9 | 6 | ⁵ | ¹ ⁵ | 8 | 4 | 2 |
| 3 | 1 | 9 | 5 | 4 | 8 | 2 | 7 | 6 | 3 | 3 |
| 4 | 7 | 5 | 6 | 2 | 9 | 1 | 3 | 4 | 8 | 4 |
| 5 | 9 | 3 | 1 | 5 | 4 | 8 | 6 | 2 | 7 | 5 |
| 6 | 8 | 4 | 2 | 6 | 3 | 7 | ¹ ⁵ ¹ | | 9 | 6 |
| 7 | 3 | 6 | 9 | 8 | 5 | 4 | 2 | 7 | 1 | 7 |
| 8 | 5 | 2 | 8 | 1 | 7 | 9 | 4 | 3 | 6 | 8 |
| 9 | 4 | 1 | 7 | 3 | 2 | 6 | 8 | 9 | 5 | 9 |

A  B  C  D  E  F  G  H  I

Puzzle 2A  Grid 8
**Final Solution**

(C) Only number missing in this box is 5.

(A) Must be 1.

(B) Only number missing in this row is 5.

(D) Only number missing in this row is 1.

(E) This cell must be 1.

(F) Cell must be 5.

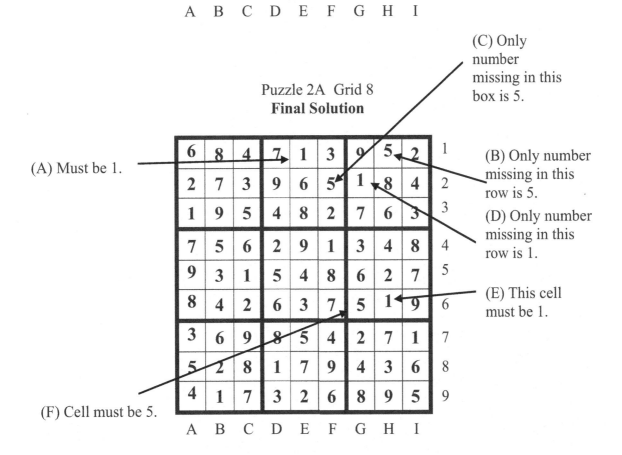

| | A | B | C | D | E | F | G | H | I | |
|---|---|---|---|---|---|---|---|---|---|---|
| 1 | 6 | 8 | 4 | 7 | 1 | 3 | 9 | 5 | 2 | 1 |
| 2 | 2 | 7 | 3 | 9 | 6 | 5 | 1 | 8 | 4 | 2 |
| 3 | 1 | 9 | 5 | 4 | 8 | 2 | 7 | 6 | 3 | 3 |
| 4 | 7 | 5 | 6 | 2 | 9 | 1 | 3 | 4 | 8 | 4 |
| 5 | 9 | 3 | 1 | 5 | 4 | 8 | 6 | 2 | 7 | 5 |
| 6 | 8 | 4 | 2 | 6 | 3 | 7 | 5 | 1 | 9 | 6 |
| 7 | 3 | 6 | 9 | 8 | 5 | 4 | 2 | 7 | 1 | 7 |
| 8 | 5 | 2 | 8 | 1 | 7 | 9 | 4 | 3 | 6 | 8 |
| 9 | 4 | 1 | 7 | 3 | 2 | 6 | 8 | 9 | 5 | 9 |

A  B  C  D  E  F  G  H  I

## Worksheet for Puzzle 3

Cut along the dotted line to remove the worksheet.

| 8 |   | 5 |   |   |   | 1 |   | 2 |
|---|---|---|---|---|---|---|---|---|
|   |   |   | 7 |   | 5 |   |   |   |
|   | 7 | 3 |   | 2 |   | 5 | 6 |   |
|   |   |   | 3 | 2 |   |   |   |   |
|   | 4 | 2 |   |   |   | 9 | 1 |   |
|   |   |   | 4 |   | 6 |   |   |   |
|   | 8 | 4 |   | 6 |   | 7 | 3 |   |
|   |   |   | 1 |   | 8 |   |   |   |
| 1 |   | 9 |   |   |   | 2 |   | 6 |

## Puzzle 3

This puzzle is more challenging. Follow the solution process step by step. Work in progression from Step A through G, referring back to Grid 1 to verify open cells.

Puzzle 3  Grid 1

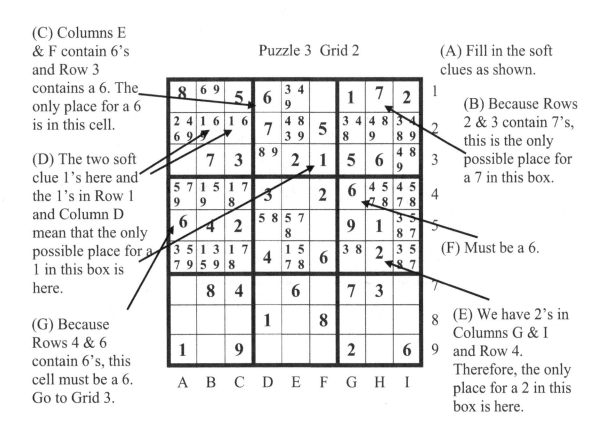

Puzzle 3  Grid 2

(C) Columns E & F contain 6's and Row 3 contains a 6. The only place for a 6 is in this cell.

(D) The two soft clue 1's here and the 1's in Row 1 and Column D mean that the only possible place for a 1 in this box is here.

(G) Because Rows 4 & 6 contain 6's, this cell must be a 6. Go to Grid 3.

(A) Fill in the soft clues as shown.

(B) Because Rows 2 & 3 contain 7's, this is the only possible place for a 7 in this box.

(F) Must be a 6.

(E) We have 2's in Columns G & I and Row 4. Therefore, the only place for a 2 in this box is here.

61

## Grid 2

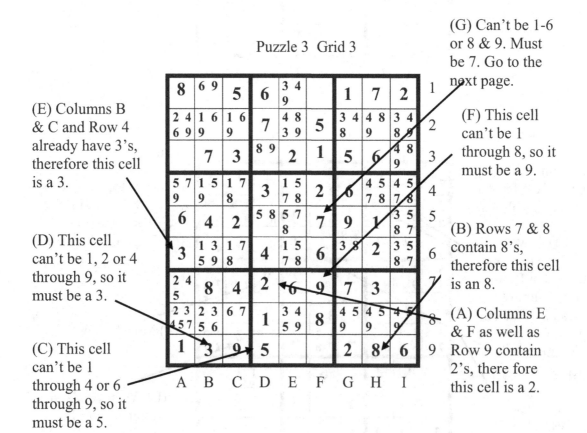

## Puzzle 3  Grid 3

(E) Columns B & C and Row 4 already have 3's, therefore this cell is a 3.

(D) This cell can't be 1, 2 or 4 through 9, so it must be a 3.

(C) This cell can't be 1 through 4 or 6 through 9, so it must be a 5.

(G) Can't be 1-6 or 8 & 9. Must be 7. Go to the next page.

(F) This cell can't be 1 through 8, so it must be a 9.

(B) Rows 7 & 8 contain 8's, therefore this cell is an 8.

(A) Columns E & F as well as Row 9 contain 2's, there fore this cell is a 2.

Grid 3

| | A | B | C | D | E | F | G | H | I | |
|---|---|---|---|---|---|---|---|---|---|---|
| 1 | 8 | 6 9 | 5 | 6 | 3 4 9 | | 1 | 7 | 2 | 1 |
| 2 | 2 4 6 9 | 1 6 9 | 1 6 9 | 7 | 4 8 3 9 | 5 | 3 4 8 | 4 8 9 | 3 4 8 9 | 2 |
| 3 | | 7 | 3 | 8 9 | 2 | 1 | 5 | 6 | 4 8 9 | 3 |
| 4 | 5 7 9 | 1 5 9 | 1 7 8 | 3 | 1 5 7 8 | 2 | 6 | 4 5 7 8 | 4 5 7 8 | 4 |
| 5 | 6 | 4 | 2 | 5 8 | 5 7 8 | 7 | 9 | 1 | 3 5 8 7 | 5 |
| 6 | 3 | 1 3 5 9 | 1 7 8 | 4 | 1 5 7 8 | 6 | 3 8 | 2 | 3 5 8 7 | 6 |
| 7 | 2 4 5 | 8 | 4 | 2 | 6 | 9 | 7 | 3 | | 7 |
| 8 | 2 3 4 5 7 | 2 3 5 6 | 6 7 | 1 | 3 4 5 9 | 8 | 4 5 9 | 4 5 9 | 4 5 9 | 8 |
| 9 | 1 | 3 | 9 | 5 | | | 2 | 8 | 6 | 9 |

A  B  C  D  E  F  G  H  I

Puzzle 3  Grid 4

(A) Can't be 1 through 8. Must be 9.

(E) The only number need in this row is a 4.

(F) Columns B & C contain 9's, therefore this cell must be a 9. Go to Grid 5.

(B) Two soft clue 7's in the left bottom box, Row 8, and a 7 in Column F are given. Therefore, this cell must be a 7.

(D) 3 is the only number missing in this column.

(C) Three soft clue 4's are in the right bottom box, Row 8 and a 4 in Column D. Therefore, this cell must be a 4.

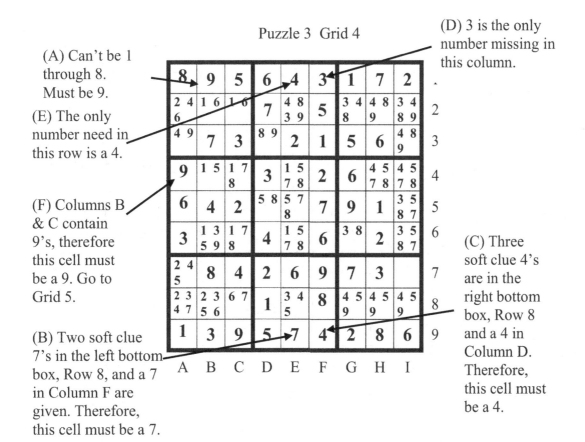

63

**Grid 4**

| A | B | C | D | E | F | G | H | I | |
|---|---|---|---|---|---|---|---|---|---|
| 8 | 9 | 5 | 6 | 4 | 3 | 1 | 7 | 2 | 1 |
| 2 4 6 | 1 6 | 1 6 | 7 | 4 8 3 9 | 5 | 3 4 8 | 4 8 9 | 3 4 8 9 | 2 |
| 4 9 | 7 | 3 | 8 9 | 2 | 1 | 5 | 6 | 4 8 9 | 3 |
| 9 | 1 5 | 1 7 8 | 3 | 1 5 7 8 | 2 | 6 | 4 5 7 8 | 4 5 7 8 | 4 |
| 6 | 4 | 2 | 5 8 | 5 7 8 | 7 | 9 | 1 | 3 5 8 7 | 5 |
| 3 | 1 3 5 9 | 1 7 8 | 4 | 1 5 7 8 | 6 | 3 8 | 2 | 3 5 8 7 | 6 |
| 2 4 5 | 8 | 4 | 2 | 6 | 9 | 7 | 3 | | 7 |
| 2 3 4 7 | 2 3 5 6 | 6 7 | 1 | 3 4 5 | 8 | 4 5 9 | 4 5 9 | 4 5 9 | 8 |
| 1 | 3 | 9 | 5 | 7 | 4 | 2 | 8 | 6 | 9 |

Puzzle 3  Grid 5

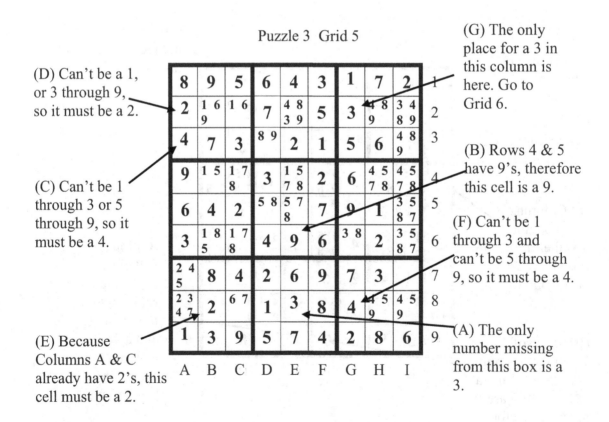

(G) The only place for a 3 in this column is here. Go to Grid 6.

(D) Can't be a 1, or 3 through 9, so it must be a 2.

(C) Can't be 1 through 3 or 5 through 9, so it must be a 4.

(B) Rows 4 & 5 have 9's, therefore this cell is a 9.

(F) Can't be 1 through 3 and can't be 5 through 9, so it must be a 4.

(E) Because Columns A & C already have 2's, this cell must be a 2.

(A) The only number missing from this box is a 3.

Grid 5

| | A | B | C | D | E | F | G | H | I | |
|---|---|---|---|---|---|---|---|---|---|---|
| 1 | 8 | 9 | 5 | 6 | 4 | 3 | 1 | 7 | 2 | 1 |
| 2 | 2 | 1 6 9 | 1 6 | 7 | 4 8 3 9 | 5 | 3 | 4 8 9 | 3 4 8 9 | 2 |
| 3 | 4 | 7 | 3 | 8 9 | 2 | 1 | 5 | 6 | 4 8 9 | 3 |
| 4 | 9 | 1 5 | 1 7 8 | 3 | 1 5 7 8 | 2 | 6 | 4 5 7 8 | 4 5 7 8 | 4 |
| 5 | 6 | 4 | 2 | 5 8 | 5 7 8 | 7 | 9 | 1 | 3 5 8 7 | 5 |
| 6 | 3 | 1 8 5 | 1 7 8 | 4 | 9 | 6 | 3 8 | 2 | 3 5 8 7 | 6 |
| 7 | 2 4 5 | 8 | 4 | 2 | 6 | 9 | 7 | 3 | | 7 |
| 8 | 2 3 4 7 | 2 | 6 7 | 1 | 3 | 8 | 4 | 4 5 9 | 4 5 9 | 8 |
| 9 | 1 | 3 | 9 | 5 | 7 | 4 | 2 | 8 | 6 | 9 |

A B C D E F G H I

Puzzle 3  Grid 6

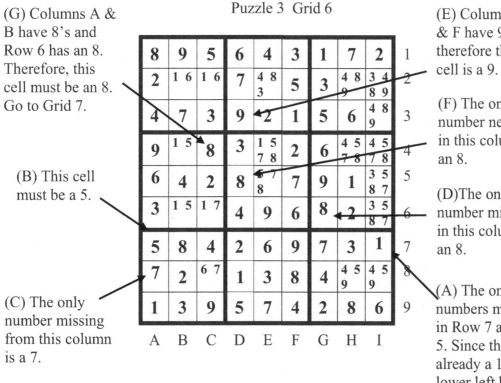

(G) Columns A & B have 8's and Row 6 has an 8. Therefore, this cell must be an 8. Go to Grid 7.

(B) This cell must be a 5.

(C) The only number missing from this column is a 7.

(E) Columns E & F have 9's, therefore this cell is a 9.

(F) The only number needed in this column is an 8.

(D) The only number missing in this column is an 8.

(A) The only numbers missing in Row 7 are 1 & 5. Since there is already a 1 in the lower left box, this cell is a 1.

65

Grid 6

|   | A | B | C | D | E | F | G | H | I |   |
|---|---|---|---|---|---|---|---|---|---|---|
| 1 | 8 | 9 | 5 | 6 | 4 | 3 | 1 | 7 | 2 | 1 |
| 2 | 2 | 1 6 | 1 6 | 7 | 4 8 3 | 5 | 3 | 4 8 9 | 3 4 8 9 | 2 |
| 3 | 4 | 7 | 3 | 9 | 2 | 1 | 5 | 6 | 4 8 9 | 3 |
| 4 | 9 | 1 5 | 8 | 3 | 1 5 7 8 | 2 | 6 | 4 5 7 8 | 4 5 7 8 | 4 |
| 5 | 6 | 4 | 2 | 8 | 5 7 8 | 7 | 9 | 1 | 3 5 8 7 | 5 |
| 6 | 3 | 1 5 | 1 7 | 4 | 9 | 6 | 8 | 2 | 3 5 8 7 | 6 |
| 7 | 5 | 8 | 4 | 2 | 6 | 9 | 7 | 3 | 1 | 7 |
| 8 | 7 | 2 | 6 7 | 1 | 3 | 8 | 4 | 4 5 9 | 4 5 9 | 8 |
| 9 | 1 | 3 | 9 | 5 | 7 | 4 | 2 | 8 | 6 | 9 |

Puzzle 3  Grid 7

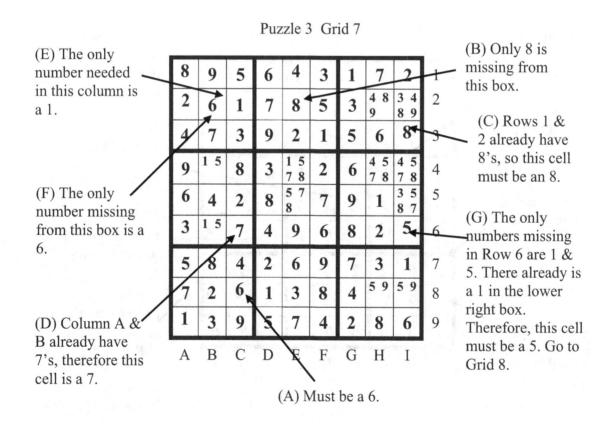

(E) The only number needed in this column is a 1.

(F) The only number missing from this box is a 6.

(D) Column A & B already have 7's, therefore this cell is a 7.

(A) Must be a 6.

(B) Only 8 is missing from this box.

(C) Rows 1 & 2 already have 8's, so this cell must be an 8.

(G) The only numbers missing in Row 6 are 1 & 5. There already is a 1 in the lower right box. Therefore, this cell must be a 5. Go to Grid 8.

66

## Grid 7

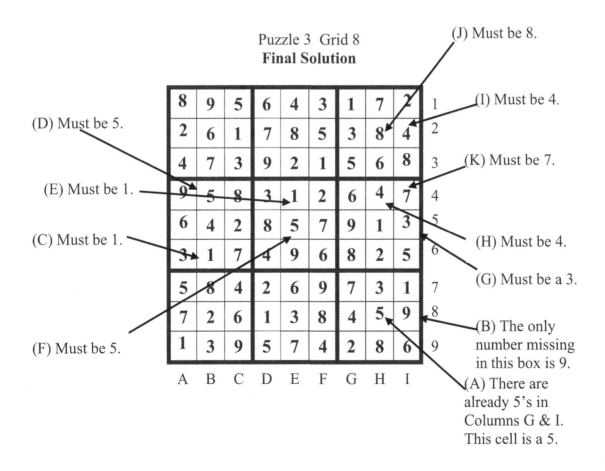

| | | | | | | | | | |
|---|---|---|---|---|---|---|---|---|---|
| 8 | 9 | 5 | 6 | 4 | 3 | 1 | 7 | 2 | 1 |
| 2 | 6 | 1 | 7 | 8 | 5 | 3 | 4 8 9 | 3 4 8 9 | 2 |
| 4 | 7 | 3 | 9 | 2 | 1 | 5 | 6 | 8 | 3 |
| 9 | 1 5 | 8 | 3 | 1 5 7 8 | 2 | 6 | 4 5 7 8 | 4 5 7 8 | 4 |
| 6 | 4 | 2 | 8 | 5 7 8 | 7 | 9 | 1 | 3 5 8 7 | 5 |
| 3 | 1 5 | 7 | 4 | 9 | 6 | 8 | 2 | 5 | 6 |
| 5 | 8 | 4 | 2 | 6 | 9 | 7 | 3 | 1 | 7 |
| 7 | 2 | 6 | 1 | 3 | 8 | 4 | 5 9 | 5 9 | 8 |
| 1 | 3 | 9 | 5 | 7 | 4 | 2 | 8 | 6 | 9 |

A  B  C  D  E  F  G  H  I

## Puzzle 3  Grid 8
### Final Solution

(J) Must be 8.

(D) Must be 5.

(I) Must be 4.

(E) Must be 1.

(K) Must be 7.

(C) Must be 1.

(H) Must be 4.

(G) Must be a 3.

(F) Must be 5.

(B) The only number missing in this box is 9.

(A) There are already 5's in Columns G & I. This cell is a 5.

| | | | | | | | | | |
|---|---|---|---|---|---|---|---|---|---|
| 8 | 9 | 5 | 6 | 4 | 3 | 1 | 7 | 2 | 1 |
| 2 | 6 | 1 | 7 | 8 | 5 | 3 | 8 | 4 | 2 |
| 4 | 7 | 3 | 9 | 2 | 1 | 5 | 6 | 8 | 3 |
| 9 | 5 | 8 | 3 | 1 | 2 | 6 | 4 | 7 | 4 |
| 6 | 4 | 2 | 8 | 5 | 7 | 9 | 1 | 3 | 5 |
| 3 | 1 | 7 | 4 | 9 | 6 | 8 | 2 | 5 | 6 |
| 5 | 8 | 4 | 2 | 6 | 9 | 7 | 3 | 1 | 7 |
| 7 | 2 | 6 | 1 | 3 | 8 | 4 | 5 | 9 | 8 |
| 1 | 3 | 9 | 5 | 7 | 4 | 2 | 8 | 6 | 9 |

A  B  C  D  E  F  G  H  I

## Worksheet for Puzzle 4

Cut along the dotted line to remove the worksheet.

| 8 | 2 |   |   |   |   | 6 | 1 |   |
|---|---|---|---|---|---|---|---|---|
| 3 |   |   | 2 |   |   | 7 |   |   |
| 1 |   | 9 | 8 |   | 6 |   |   |   |
| 2 |   |   | 4 |   |   |   |   |   |
|   |   | 8 | 7 |   | 9 | 5 |   |   |
|   |   |   |   |   | 3 |   |   | 1 |
|   |   |   | 9 |   | 4 | 1 |   | 3 |
|   |   | 7 |   |   | 5 |   |   | 2 |
|   | 4 | 3 |   |   |   |   | 5 | 8 |

## Puzzle 4

Number of given clues – 30. Here is another more complex puzzle. The pace will increase slightly.

Puzzle 4  Grid 1

|   | A | B | C | D | E | F | G | H | I |   |
|---|---|---|---|---|---|---|---|---|---|---|
| 1 | 8 | 2 |   |   |   |   | 6 | 1 |   | 1 |
| 2 | 3 |   |   | 2 |   |   | 7 |   |   | 2 |
| 3 | 1 |   | 9 | 8 |   | 6 |   |   |   | 3 |
| 4 | 2 |   |   | 4 |   |   |   |   |   | 4 |
| 5 |   |   | 8 | 7 |   | 9 | 5 |   |   | 5 |
| 6 |   |   |   |   |   | 3 |   |   | 1 | 6 |
| 7 |   |   |   | 9 |   | 4 | 1 |   | 3 | 7 |
| 8 |   |   | 7 |   |   | 5 |   |   | 2 | 8 |
| 9 |   | 4 | 3 |   |   |   |   | 5 | 8 | 9 |

A   B   C   D   E   F   G   H   I

(A) Fill in all the soft clues possible and then start working on the hard clues.

(B) Can't be 1-6 and can't be 8 or 9. Must be 7.

(G) This cell must be a 2 because there are 2's in columns A & B. Go to next page.

Puzzle 4  Grid 2

(D) This cell must contain an 8.

(C) This cell must contain a 1.

(E) This cell must be a 1.

(F) Use the listing technique to solve for this cell. Now count from one to nine. This cell must be a 9.

Grid 2

71

Puzzle 4  Grid 3

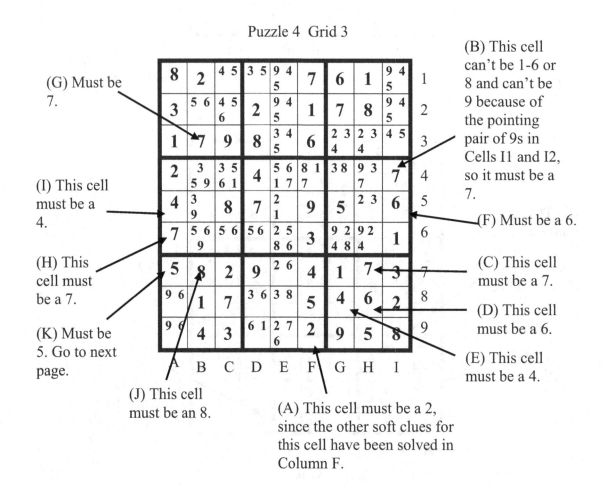

(G) Must be 7.

(I) This cell must be a 4.

(H) This cell must be a 7.

(K) Must be 5. Go to next page.

(J) This cell must be an 8.

(B) This cell can't be 1-6 or 8 and can't be 9 because of the pointing pair of 9s in Cells I1 and I2, so it must be a 7.

(F) Must be a 6.

(C) This cell must be a 7.

(D) This cell must be a 6.

(E) This cell must be a 4.

(A) This cell must be a 2, since the other soft clues for this cell have been solved in Column F.

72

## Grid 3

| | A | B | C | D | E | F | G | H | I | |
|---|---|---|---|---|---|---|---|---|---|---|
| 1 | 8 | 2 | 4 5 | 3 5 | 9 4 5 | 7 | 6 | 1 | 9 4 5 | 1 |
| 2 | 3 | 5 6 | 4 5 6 | 2 | 9 4 5 | 1 | 7 | 8 | 9 4 5 | 2 |
| 3 | 1 | 7 | 9 | 8 | 3 4 5 | 6 | 2 3 4 | 2 3 4 | 4 5 | 3 |
| 4 | 2 | 3 5 9 | 3 5 6 1 | 4 | 5 6 1 7 | 8 1 7 | 3 8 | 9 3 7 | 7 | 4 |
| 5 | 4 | 3 9 | 8 | 7 | 2 1 | 9 | 5 | 2 3 | 6 | 5 |
| 6 | 7 | 5 6 9 | 5 6 | 5 6 | 2 5 8 6 | 3 | 9 2 4 8 | 9 2 4 | 1 | 6 |
| 7 | 5 | 8 | 2 | 9 | 2 6 | 4 | 1 | 7 | 3 | 7 |
| 8 | 9 6 | 1 | 7 | 3 6 | 3 8 | 5 | 4 | 6 | 2 | 8 |
| 9 | 9 6 | 4 | 3 | 6 1 | 2 7 6 | 2 | 9 | 5 | 8 | 9 |

## Puzzle 4 Grid 4

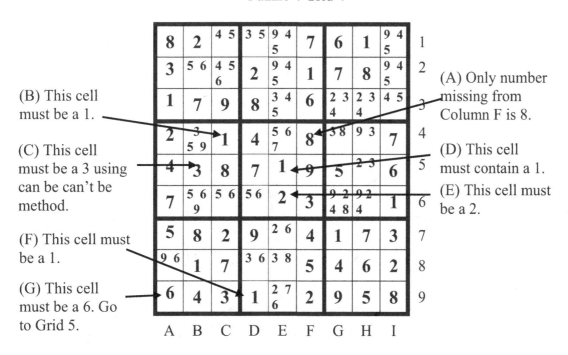

(B) This cell must be a 1.

(C) This cell must be a 3 using can be can't be method.

(F) This cell must be a 1.

(G) This cell must be a 6. Go to Grid 5.

(A) Only number missing from Column F is 8.

(D) This cell must contain a 1.

(E) This cell must be a 2.

Grid 4

| | A | B | C | D | E | F | G | H | I | |
|---|---|---|---|---|---|---|---|---|---|---|
| 1 | 8 | 2 | 4 5 | 3 5 | 9 4 5 | 7 | 6 | 1 | 9 4 5 | 1 |
| 2 | 3 | 5 6 | 4 5 6 | 2 | 9 4 5 | 1 | 7 | 8 | 9 4 5 | 2 |
| 3 | 1 | 7 | 9 | 8 | 3 4 5 | 6 | 2 3 4 | 2 3 4 | 4 5 | 3 |
| 4 | 2 | 3 5 9 | 1 | 4 | 5 6 7 | 8 | 3 8 | 9 3 | 7 | 4 |
| 5 | 4 | 3 | 8 | 7 | 1 | 9 | 5 | 2 3 | 6 | 5 |
| 6 | 7 | 5 6 9 | 5 6 | 5 6 | 2 | 3 | 9 2 4 8 | 9 2 4 | 1 | 6 |
| 7 | 5 | 8 | 2 | 9 | 2 6 | 4 | 1 | 7 | 3 | 7 |
| 8 | 9 6 | 1 | 7 | 3 6 | 3 8 | 5 | 4 | 6 | 2 | 8 |
| 9 | 6 | 4 | 3 | 1 | 2 7 6 | 2 | 9 | 5 | 8 | 9 |

Puzzle 4  Grid 5

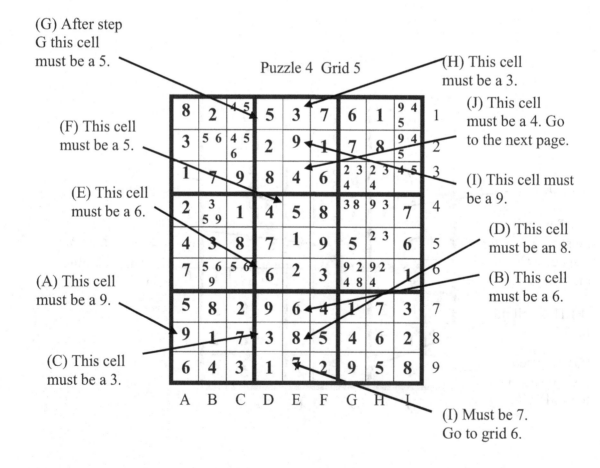

(G) After step G this cell must be a 5.

(H) This cell must be a 3.

(F) This cell must be a 5.

(J) This cell must be a 4. Go to the next page.

(E) This cell must be a 6.

(I) This cell must be a 9.

(D) This cell must be an 8.

(A) This cell must be a 9.

(B) This cell must be a 6.

(C) This cell must be a 3.

(I) Must be 7. Go to grid 6.

74

Grid 5

| | A | B | C | D | E | F | G | H | I | |
|---|---|---|---|---|---|---|---|---|---|---|
| 1 | 8 | 2 | 4 5 | 5 | 3 | 7 | 6 | 1 | 9 4 5 | 1 |
| 2 | 3 | 5 6 | 4 5 6 | 2 | 9 | 1 | 7 | 8 | 9 4 5 | 2 |
| 3 | 1 | 7 | 9 | 8 | 4 | 6 | 2 3 4 | 2 3 4 | 4 5 | 3 |
| 4 | 2 | 3 5 9 | 1 | 4 | 5 | 8 | 3 8 | 9 3 | 7 | 4 |
| 5 | 4 | 3 | 8 | 7 | 1 | 9 | 5 | 2 3 | 6 | 5 |
| 6 | 7 | 5 6 9 | 5 6 | 6 | 2 | 3 | 9 2 4 8 | 9 2 4 | 1 | 6 |
| 7 | 5 | 8 | 2 | 9 | 6 | 4 | 1 | 7 | 3 | 7 |
| 8 | 9 | 1 | 7 | 3 | 8 | 5 | 4 | 6 | 2 | 8 |
| 9 | 6 | 4 | 3 | 1 | 7 | 2 | 9 | 5 | 8 | 9 |

A  B  C  D  E  F  G  H  I

Puzzle 4  Grid 6

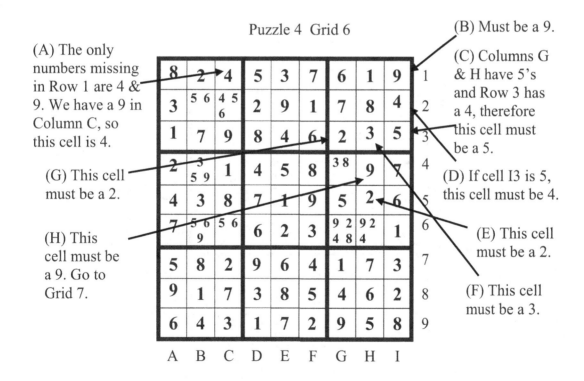

(A) The only numbers missing in Row 1 are 4 & 9. We have a 9 in Column C, so this cell is 4.

(B) Must be a 9.

(C) Columns G & H have 5's and Row 3 has a 4, therefore this cell must be a 5.

(D) If cell I3 is 5, this cell must be 4.

(E) This cell must be a 2.

(F) This cell must be a 3.

(G) This cell must be a 2.

(H) This cell must be a 9. Go to Grid 7.

75

Grid 6

Puzzle 4 Grid 7
**Final Solution**

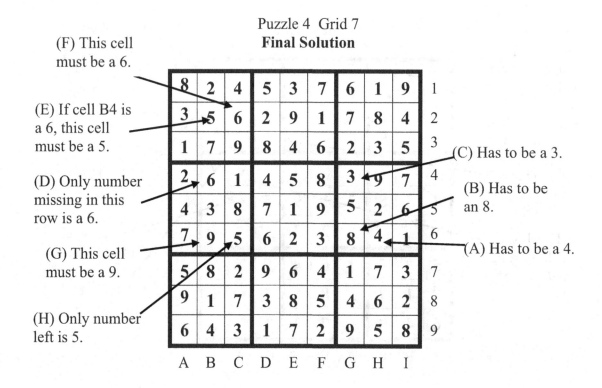

(F) This cell must be a 6.

(E) If cell B4 is a 6, this cell must be a 5.

(D) Only number missing in this row is a 6.

(G) This cell must be a 9.

(H) Only number left is 5.

(C) Has to be a 3.

(B) Has to be an 8.

(A) Has to be a 4.

## Worksheet for Puzzle 5

Cut along the dotted line to remove the worksheet.

| | 5 | 2 | | 8 | 3 | 1 | 4 | |
|---|---|---|---|---|---|---|---|---|
| | | | | | | | | |
| 9 | 4 | | | | 7 | 3 | 2 | |
| | | 8 | | | 1 | | | |
| | 3 | 1 | | | | 7 | 6 | |
| | | | 7 | | | 5 | | |
| | 6 | 7 | 5 | | | | 1 | 9 |
| | | | | | | | | |
| | 9 | 4 | 6 | 7 | | 8 | 3 | |

## Puzzle 5

Puzzle 5  Grid 1

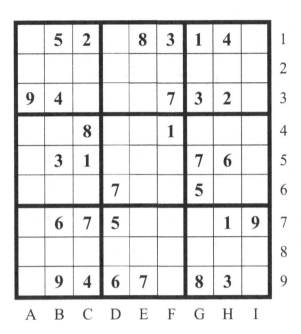

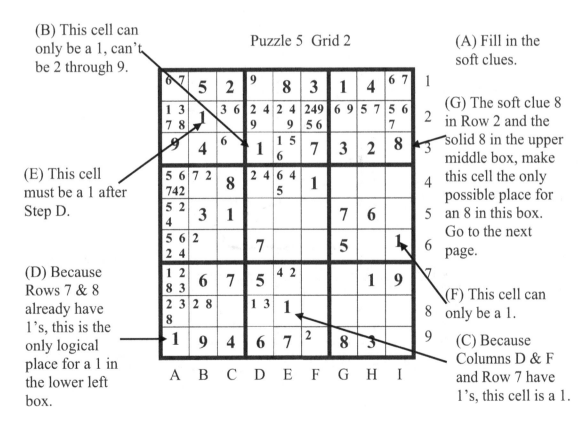

(B) This cell can only be a 1, can't be 2 through 9.

Puzzle 5  Grid 2

(A) Fill in the soft clues.

(E) This cell must be a 1 after Step D.

(D) Because Rows 7 & 8 already have 1's, this is the only logical place for a 1 in the lower left box.

(G) The soft clue 8 in Row 2 and the solid 8 in the upper middle box, make this cell the only possible place for an 8 in this box. Go to the next page.

(F) This cell can only be a 1.

(C) Because Columns D & F and Row 7 have 1's, this cell is a 1.

## Grid 2

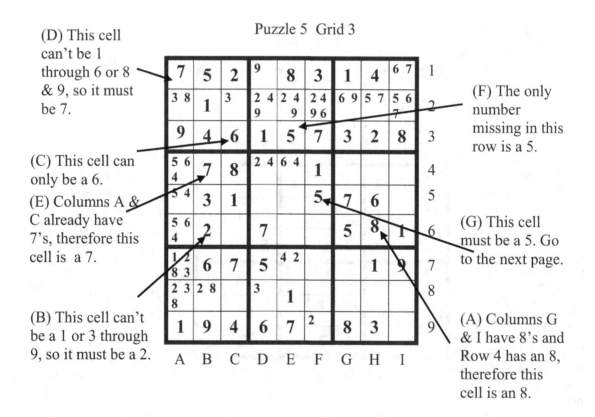

---

# Puzzle 5 Grid 3

(D) This cell can't be 1 through 6 or 8 & 9, so it must be 7.

(F) The only number missing in this row is a 5.

(C) This cell can only be a 6.

(E) Columns A & C already have 7's, therefore this cell is a 7.

(G) This cell must be a 5. Go to the next page.

(B) This cell can't be a 1 or 3 through 9, so it must be a 2.

(A) Columns G & I have 8's and Row 4 has an 8, therefore this cell is an 8.

Grid 3

Puzzle 5  Grid 4

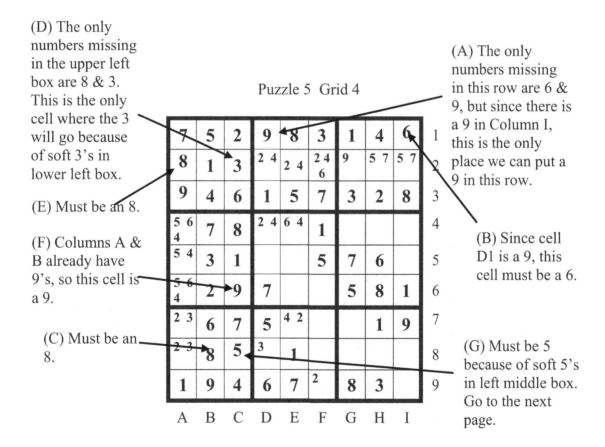

(D) The only numbers missing in the upper left box are 8 & 3. This is the only cell where the 3 will go because of soft 3's in lower left box.

(E) Must be an 8.

(F) Columns A & B already have 9's, so this cell is a 9.

(C) Must be an 8.

(A) The only numbers missing in this row are 6 & 9, but since there is a 9 in Column I, this is the only place we can put a 9 in this row.

(B) Since cell D1 is a 9, this cell must be a 6.

(G) Must be 5 because of soft 5's in left middle box. Go to the next page.

81

Grid 4

| | A | B | C | D | E | F | G | H | I | |
|---|---|---|---|---|---|---|---|---|---|---|
| 1 | 7 | 5 | 2 | 9 | 8 | 3 | 1 | 4 | 6 | 1 |
| 2 | 8 | 1 | 3 | 2 4 | 2 4 | 2 4 6 | 9 | 5 7 | 5 7 | 2 |
| 3 | 9 | 4 | 6 | 1 | 5 | 7 | 3 | 2 | 8 | 3 |
| 4 | 5 6 4 | 7 | 8 | 2 4 6 4 | 1 | | | | | 4 |
| 5 | 5 4 | 3 | 1 | | | 5 | 7 | 6 | | 5 |
| 6 | 5 6 4 | 2 | 9 | 7 | | | 5 | 8 | 1 | 6 |
| 7 | 2 3 | 6 | 7 | 5 | 4 2 | | | 1 | 9 | 7 |
| 8 | 2 3 | 8 | 5 | 3 | 1 | | | | | 8 |
| 9 | 1 | 9 | 4 | 6 | 7 | 2 | 8 | 3 | | 9 |

A  B  C  D  E  F  G  H  I

Puzzle 5  Grid 5

(A) Columns B & C and Rows 5 & 6 have 5's, so this cell must be a 5.

(E) Must be a 9.

(F) Columns I & G have 9's, so this cell is a 9. Go to the next page.

(D) Only number missing in Row 9 is 2.

(B) Columns H & I and Row 7 have 6's, so this cell is a 6.

(C) Must be 5.

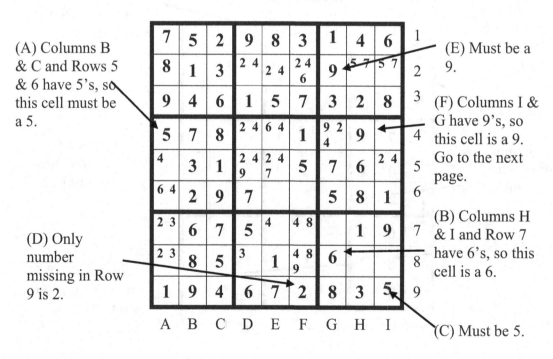

| | A | B | C | D | E | F | G | H | I | |
|---|---|---|---|---|---|---|---|---|---|---|
| 1 | 7 | 5 | 2 | 9 | 8 | 3 | 1 | 4 | 6 | 1 |
| 2 | 8 | 1 | 3 | 2 4 | 2 4 | 2 4 6 | 9 | 5 7 | 5 7 | 2 |
| 3 | 9 | 4 | 6 | 1 | 5 | 7 | 3 | 2 | 8 | 3 |
| 4 | 5 | 7 | 8 | 2 4 6 4 | 1 | | 9 2 4 | 9 | | 4 |
| 5 | 4 | 3 | 1 | 2 4 9 | 2 4 7 | 5 | 7 | 6 | 2 4 | 5 |
| 6 | 6 4 | 2 | 9 | 7 | | | 5 | 8 | 1 | 6 |
| 7 | 2 3 | 6 | 7 | 5 | 4 | 4 8 | | 1 | 9 | 7 |
| 8 | 2 3 | 8 | 5 | 3 | 1 | 4 8 9 | 6 | | | 8 |
| 9 | 1 | 9 | 4 | 6 | 7 | 2 | 8 | 3 | 5 | 9 |

A  B  C  D  E  F  G  H  I

82

Grid 5

| | | | | | | | | | |
|---|---|---|---|---|---|---|---|---|---|
| 7 | 5 | 2 | 9 | 8 | 3 | 1 | 4 | 6 | 1 |
| 8 | 1 | 3 | 2 4 | 2 4 | 2 4 6 | 9 | 5 7 | 5 7 | 2 |
| 9 | 4 | 6 | 1 | 5 | 7 | 3 | 2 | 8 | 3 |
| 5 | 7 | 8 | 2 4 6 4 | 1 | 9 2 4 | 9 | | | 4 |
| 4 | 3 | 1 | 2 4 9 | 2 4 7 | 5 | 7 | 6 | 2 4 | 5 |
| 6 4 | 2 | 9 | 7 | | | 5 | 8 | 1 | 6 |
| 2 3 | 6 | 7 | 5 | 4 | 4 8 | | 1 | 9 | 7 |
| 2 3 | 8 | 5 | 3 | 1 | 4 8 9 | 6 | | | 8 |
| 1 | 9 | 4 | 6 | 7 | 2 | 8 | 3 | 5 | 9 |

A  B  C  D  E  F  G  H  I

Puzzle 5  Grid 6

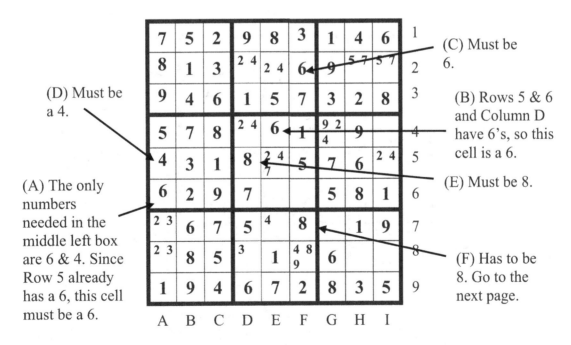

(C) Must be 6.

(D) Must be a 4.

(B) Rows 5 & 6 and Column D have 6's, so this cell is a 6.

(E) Must be 8.

(A) The only numbers needed in the middle left box are 6 & 4. Since Row 5 already has a 6, this cell must be a 6.

(F) Has to be 8. Go to the next page.

A  B  C  D  E  F  G  H  I

83

Grid 6

| | A | B | C | D | E | F | G | H | I | |
|---|---|---|---|---|---|---|---|---|---|---|
| 1 | 7 | 5 | 2 | 9 | 8 | 3 | 1 | 4 | 6 | 1 |
| 2 | 8 | 1 | 3 | 2 4 | 2 4 | 6 | 9 | 5 7 | 5 7 | 2 |
| 3 | 9 | 4 | 6 | 1 | 5 | 7 | 3 | 2 | 8 | 3 |
| 4 | 5 | 7 | 8 | 2 4 | 6 | 1 | 9 2 4 | 9 | | 4 |
| 5 | 4 | 3 | 1 | 8 | 2 4 7 | 5 | 7 | 6 | 2 4 | 5 |
| 6 | 6 | 2 | 9 | 7 | | | 5 | 8 | 1 | 6 |
| 7 | 2 3 | 6 | 7 | 5 | 4 | 8 | | 1 | 9 | 7 |
| 8 | 2 3 | 8 | 5 | 3 | 1 | 4 8 9 | 6 | | | 8 |
| 9 | 1 | 9 | 4 | 6 | 7 | 2 | 8 | 3 | 5 | 9 |

Puzzle 5  Grid 7

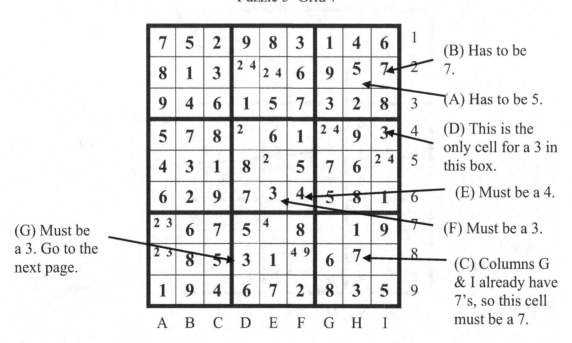

(B) Has to be 7.

(A) Has to be 5.

(D) This is the only cell for a 3 in this box.

(E) Must be a 4.

(F) Must be a 3.

(G) Must be a 3. Go to the next page.

(C) Columns G & I already have 7's, so this cell must be a 7.

84

## Grid 7

| | A | B | C | D | E | F | G | H | I | |
|---|---|---|---|---|---|---|---|---|---|---|
| | 7 | 5 | 2 | 9 | 8 | 3 | 1 | 4 | 6 | 1 |
| | 8 | 1 | 3 | 2 4 | 2 4 | 6 | 9 | 5 | 7 | 2 |
| | 9 | 4 | 6 | 1 | 5 | 7 | 3 | 2 | 8 | 3 |
| | 5 | 7 | 8 | 2 | 6 | 1 | 2 4 | 9 | 3 | 4 |
| | 4 | 3 | 1 | 8 | 2 | 5 | 7 | 6 | 2 4 | 5 |
| | 6 | 2 | 9 | 7 | 3 | 4 | 5 | 8 | 1 | 6 |
| | 2 3 | 6 | 7 | 5 | 4 | 8 | | 1 | 9 | 7 |
| | 2 3 | 8 | 5 | 3 | 1 | 4 9 | 6 | 7 | | 8 |
| | 1 | 9 | 4 | 6 | 7 | 2 | 8 | 3 | 5 | 9 |

## Puzzle 5  Grid 8

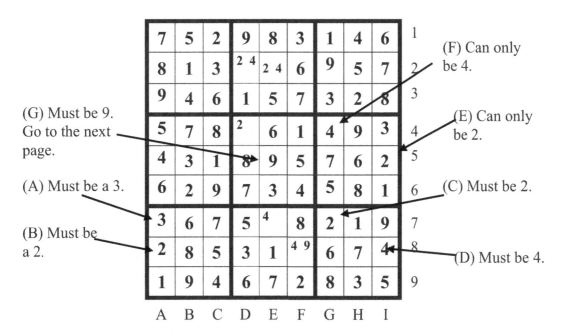

(G) Must be 9. Go to the next page.

(A) Must be a 3.

(B) Must be a 2.

(F) Can only be 4.

(E) Can only be 2.

(C) Must be 2.

(D) Must be 4.

85

Grid 8

| | A | B | C | D | E | F | G | H | I | |
|---|---|---|---|---|---|---|---|---|---|---|
| 1 | 7 | 5 | 2 | 9 | 8 | 3 | 1 | 4 | 6 | 1 |
| 2 | 8 | 1 | 3 | 2 4 | 2 4 | 6 | 9 | 5 | 7 | 2 |
| 3 | 9 | 4 | 6 | 1 | 5 | 7 | 3 | 2 | 8 | 3 |
| 4 | 5 | 7 | 8 | 2 | 6 | 1 | 4 | 9 | 3 | 4 |
| 5 | 4 | 3 | 1 | 8 | 9 | 5 | 7 | 6 | 2 | 5 |
| 6 | 6 | 2 | 9 | 7 | 3 | 4 | 5 | 8 | 1 | 6 |
| 7 | 3 | 6 | 7 | 5 | 4 | 8 | 2 | 1 | 9 | 7 |
| 8 | 2 | 8 | 5 | 3 | 1 | 4 9 | 6 | 7 | 4 | 8 |
| 9 | 1 | 9 | 4 | 6 | 7 | 2 | 8 | 3 | 5 | 9 |

A  B  C  D  E  F  G  H  I

Puzzle 5  Grid 9
**Final Solution**

(B) Must be 4.

(A) Has to be 2.

(C) Must be 2.

(D) Must be 4.

(E) Must be 9.

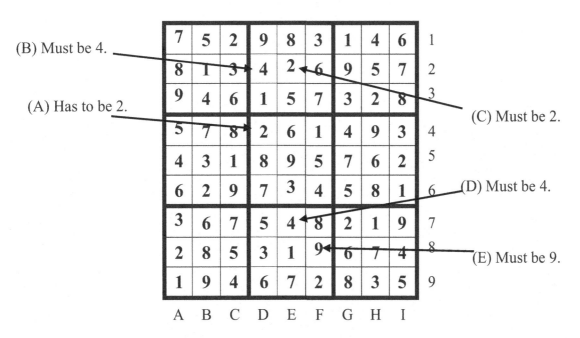

| | A | B | C | D | E | F | G | H | I | |
|---|---|---|---|---|---|---|---|---|---|---|
| 1 | 7 | 5 | 2 | 9 | 8 | 3 | 1 | 4 | 6 | 1 |
| 2 | 8 | 1 | 3 | 4 | 2 | 6 | 9 | 5 | 7 | 2 |
| 3 | 9 | 4 | 6 | 1 | 5 | 7 | 3 | 2 | 8 | 3 |
| 4 | 5 | 7 | 8 | 2 | 6 | 1 | 4 | 9 | 3 | 4 |
| 5 | 4 | 3 | 1 | 8 | 9 | 5 | 7 | 6 | 2 | 5 |
| 6 | 6 | 2 | 9 | 7 | 3 | 4 | 5 | 8 | 1 | 6 |
| 7 | 3 | 6 | 7 | 5 | 4 | 8 | 2 | 1 | 9 | 7 |
| 8 | 2 | 8 | 5 | 3 | 1 | 9 | 6 | 7 | 4 | 8 |
| 9 | 1 | 9 | 4 | 6 | 7 | 2 | 8 | 3 | 5 | 9 |

A  B  C  D  E  F  G  H  I

87

## *Worksheet for Puzzle 6*

Cut along the dotted line to remove the worksheet .

| 6 |   |   | 5 | 7 |   | 4 |   |   |
|---|---|---|---|---|---|---|---|---|
|   | 9 |   | 1 |   |   |   |   | 8 |
| 4 |   | 5 | 8 |   |   | 3 |   |   |
|   |   | 1 | 7 |   |   |   |   |   |
| 5 |   |   |   |   |   |   |   | 9 |
|   |   |   |   |   | 8 | 6 |   |   |
|   |   | 7 |   |   | 2 | 5 |   | 6 |
| 2 |   |   |   |   | 7 |   | 4 |   |
|   |   | 4 |   | 8 | 6 |   |   | 7 |

# Puzzle 6

Puzzle 6  Grid 1

|   | A | B | C | D | E | F | G | H | I |   |
|---|---|---|---|---|---|---|---|---|---|---|
| 1 | 6 |   |   | 5 | 7 |   | 4 |   |   | 1 |
| 2 |   | 9 |   | 1 |   |   |   |   | 8 | 2 |
| 3 | 4 |   | 5 | 8 |   |   | 3 |   |   | 3 |
| 4 |   |   | 1 | 7 |   |   |   |   |   | 4 |
| 5 | 5 |   |   |   |   |   |   |   | 9 | 5 |
| 6 |   |   |   |   |   | 8 | 6 |   |   | 6 |
| 7 |   |   | 7 |   |   | 2 | 5 |   | 6 | 7 |
| 8 | 2 |   |   |   |   | 7 |   | 4 |   | 8 |
| 9 |   |   | 4 |   | 8 | 6 |   |   | 7 | 9 |

A  B  C  D  E  F  G  H  I

Puzzle 6 Grid 2
Follow along steps A – G on your worksheet

(A) First fill in your soft clues.

(E) Columns D & E have 1's. This cell must be a 1.

(B) Column D and row 7 already have 5's, therefore, this cell is a 5.

(D) Column D has a 1. This cell must be a 1.

(G) The only numbers left in this column are 3, 4 – this is the only cell for 3. Go to next page.

(F) The soft 9's in Columns D & E and the 9 in Row 2 mean that this Cell is 9.

(C) Columns D & E and row 5 already have 5's – this cell is a 5.

91

## Grid 2

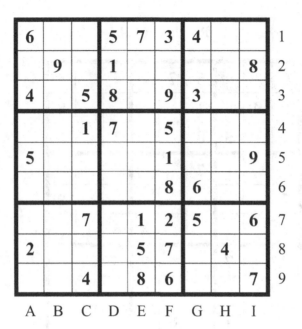

## Puzzle 6 Grid 3
Follow along steps A – G on your worksheet

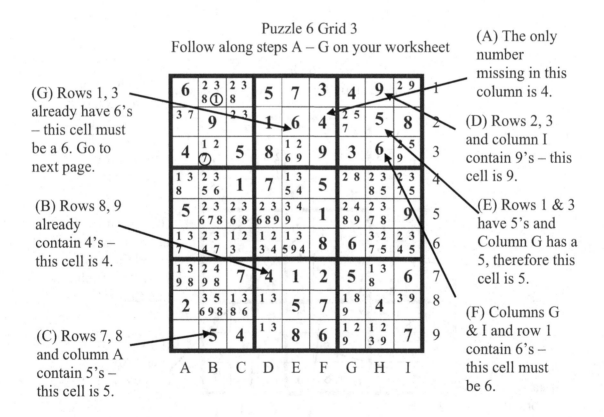

(A) The only number missing in this column is 4.

(D) Rows 2, 3 and column I contain 9's – this cell is 9.

(E) Rows 1 & 3 have 5's and Column G has a 5, therefore this cell is 5.

(F) Columns G & I and row 1 contain 6's – this cell must be 6.

(G) Rows 1, 3 already have 6's – this cell must be a 6. Go to next page.

(B) Rows 8, 9 already contain 4's – this cell is 4.

(C) Rows 7, 8 and column A contain 5's – this cell is 5.

## Grid 3

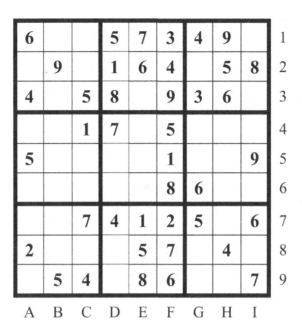

## Puzzle 6 Grid 4
## Follow along steps A – F on your worksheet

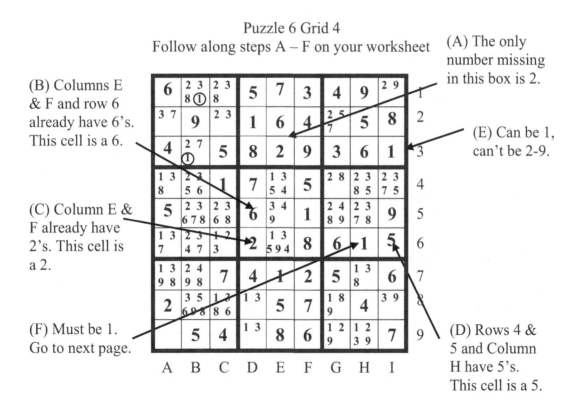

(A) The only number missing in this box is 2.

(B) Columns E & F and row 6 already have 6's. This cell is a 6.

(C) Column E & F already have 2's. This cell is a 2.

(F) Must be 1. Go to next page.

(E) Can be 1, can't be 2-9.

(D) Rows 4 & 5 and Column H have 5's. This cell is a 5.

Grid 4

| | A | B | C | D | E | F | G | H | I | |
|---|---|---|---|---|---|---|---|---|---|---|
| 1 | 6 | | | 5 | 7 | 3 | 4 | 9 | | 1 |
| 2 | | 9 | | 1 | 6 | 4 | | 5 | 8 | 2 |
| 3 | 4 | | 5 | 8 | 2 | 9 | 3 | 6 | 1 | 3 |
| 4 | | | 1 | 7 | | 5 | | | | 4 |
| 5 | 5 | | | 6 | | 1 | | | 9 | 5 |
| 6 | | | | 2 | | 8 | 6 | 1 | 5 | 6 |
| 7 | | | 7 | 4 | 1 | 2 | 5 | | 6 | 7 |
| 8 | 2 | | | | 5 | 7 | | 4 | | 8 |
| 9 | | 5 | 4 | | 8 | 6 | | | 7 | 9 |

A  B  C  D  E  F  G  H  I

## Puzzle 6 Grid 5
### Follow along steps A – H on your worksheet

(E) Rows 1 & 3 and column A have 2's. This cell is a 2.

(F) Must be 3.

(A) The only number missing in this row is 7.

(G) Must be a 6.

(B) Columns B & C and row 4 have 7's. This cell is a 7.

(D) The only number missing in this box is 2.

(C) The only numbers missing in this box are 7 and 2. 7 won't fit anywhere else but here.

(H) Columns G & I and rows 4 & 6 contain 7's. This cell is a 7. Go to next page.

94

## Grid 5

| 6 |   |   | 5 | 7 | 3 | 4 | 9 | 2 | 1 |
|---|---|---|---|---|---|---|---|---|---|
| 3 | 9 | 2 | 1 | 6 | 4 | 7 | 5 | 8 | 2 |
| 4 | 7 | 5 | 8 | 2 | 9 | 3 | 6 | 1 | 3 |
|   | 6 | 1 | 7 |   | 5 |   |   |   | 4 |
| 5 |   |   | 6 |   | 1 |   |   | 9 | 5 |
| 7 |   |   | 2 |   | 8 | 6 | 1 | 5 | 6 |
|   |   | 7 | 4 | 1 | 2 | 5 |   | 6 | 7 |
| 2 |   |   |   | 5 | 7 |   | 4 |   | 8 |
|   | 5 | 4 |   | 8 | 6 |   |   | 7 | 9 |

A  B  C  D  E  F  G  H  I

## Puzzle 6 Grid 6
### Follow along steps A – G on your worksheet

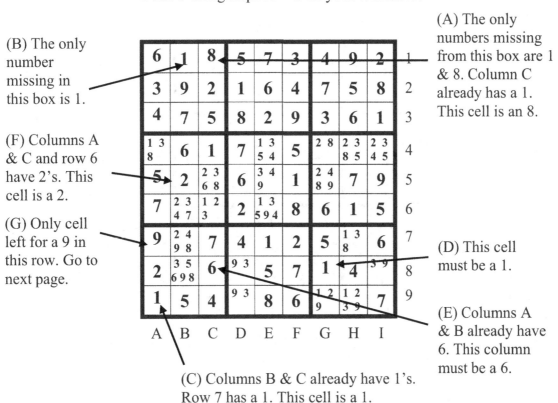

(A) The only numbers missing from this box are 1 & 8. Column C already has a 1. This cell is an 8.

(B) The only number missing in this box is 1.

(F) Columns A & C and row 6 have 2's. This cell is a 2.

(G) Only cell left for a 9 in this row. Go to next page.

(D) This cell must be a 1.

(E) Columns A & B already have 6. This column must be a 6.

(C) Columns B & C already have 1's. Row 7 has a 1. This cell is a 1.

Grid 6

Row labels 1–9 on right, column labels A–I below.

|   | A | B | C | D | E | F | G | H | I |   |
|---|---|---|---|---|---|---|---|---|---|---|
| 1 | 6 | 1 | 8 | 5 | 7 | 3 | 4 | 9 | 2 |   |
| 2 | 3 | 9 | 2 | 1 | 6 | 4 | 7 | 5 | 8 |   |
| 3 | 4 | 7 | 5 | 8 | 2 | 9 | 3 | 6 | 1 |   |
| 4 |   | 6 | 1 | 7 |   | 5 |   |   |   |   |
| 5 | 5 | 2 |   | 6 |   | 1 |   | 7 | 9 |   |
| 6 | 7 |   |   | 2 |   | 8 | 6 | 1 | 5 |   |
| 7 | 9 |   | 7 | 4 | 1 | 2 | 5 |   | 6 |   |
| 8 | 2 |   | 6 |   | 5 | 7 | 1 | 4 |   |   |
| 9 | 1 | 5 | 4 |   | 8 | 6 |   |   | 7 |   |

Puzzle 6 Grid 7
Follow along steps A – G on your worksheet

(A) Only number missing in this column is 8.

(F) This cell has to be 4.

(D) Columns A & C contain 4's. This cell is a 4.

(E) Columns G & H have 4's. This cell is a 4.

(B) Rows 4 & 6 already have 8's. This cell is an 8.

(C) Columns G & I and row 9 contain 8's. This cell is an 8.

(G) Must be a 3. Go to next page.

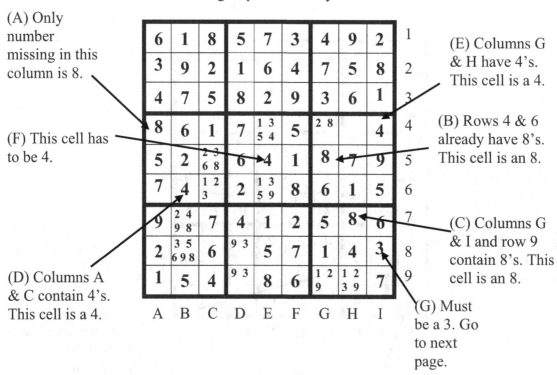

96

## Grid 7

| | A | B | C | D | E | F | G | H | I | |
|---|---|---|---|---|---|---|---|---|---|---|
| 1 | 6 | 1 | 8 | 5 | 7 | 3 | 4 | 9 | 2 | 1 |
| 2 | 3 | 9 | 2 | 1 | 6 | 4 | 7 | 5 | 8 | 2 |
| 3 | 4 | 7 | 5 | 8 | 2 | 9 | 3 | 6 | 1 | 3 |
| 4 | 8 | 6 | 1 | 7 |   | 5 |   |   | 4 | 4 |
| 5 | 5 | 2 |   | 6 | 4 | 1 | 8 | 7 | 9 | 5 |
| 6 | 7 | 4 |   | 2 |   | 8 | 6 | 1 | 5 | 6 |
| 7 | 9 |   | 7 | 4 | 1 | 2 | 5 | 8 | 6 | 7 |
| 8 | 2 |   | 6 |   | 5 | 7 | 1 | 4 | 3 | 8 |
| 9 | 1 | 5 | 4 |   | 8 | 6 |   |   | 7 | 9 |

(column labels below: A  B  C  D  E  F  G  H  I)

## Puzzle 6 Grid 8
### Follow along steps A – G on your worksheet

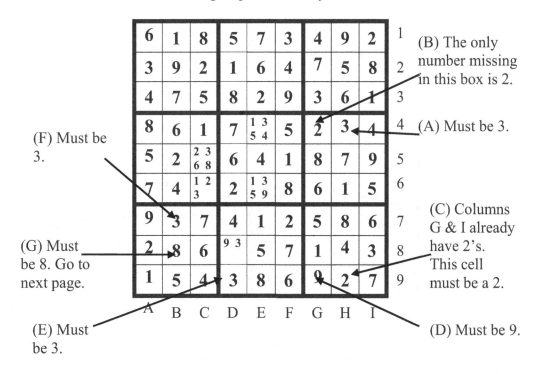

(B) The only number missing in this box is 2.

(A) Must be 3.

(F) Must be 3.

(C) Columns G & I already have 2's. This cell must be a 2.

(G) Must be 8. Go to next page.

(E) Must be 3.

(D) Must be 9.

97

## Grid 8

| 6 | 1 | 8 | 5 | 7 | 3 | 4 | 9 | 2 | 1 |
|---|---|---|---|---|---|---|---|---|---|
| 3 | 9 | 2 | 1 | 6 | 4 | 7 | 5 | 8 | 2 |
| 4 | 7 | 5 | 8 | 2 | 9 | 3 | 6 | 1 | 3 |
| 8 | 6 | 1 | 7 |   | 5 | 2 | 3 | 4 | 4 |
| 5 | 2 |   | 6 | 4 | 1 | 8 | 7 | 9 | 5 |
| 7 | 4 |   | 2 |   | 8 | 6 | 1 | 5 | 6 |
| 9 | 3 | 7 | 4 | 1 | 2 | 5 | 8 | 6 | 7 |
| 2 | 8 | 6 |   | 5 | 7 | 1 | 4 | 3 | 8 |
| 1 | 5 | 4 | 3 | 8 | 6 | 9 | 2 | 7 | 9 |

A  B  C  D  E  F  G  H  I

## Puzzle 6 Grid 9
**Final Solution**

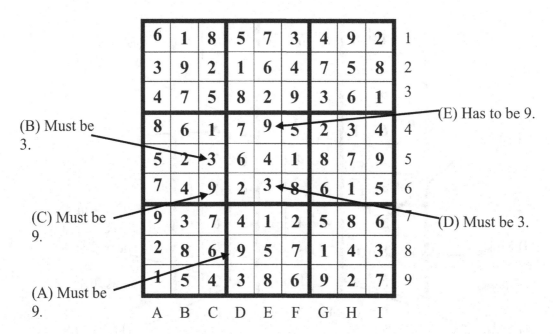

(B) Must be 3.

(C) Must be 9.

(A) Must be 9.

(E) Has to be 9.

(D) Must be 3.

| 6 | 1 | 8 | 5 | 7 | 3 | 4 | 9 | 2 | 1 |
|---|---|---|---|---|---|---|---|---|---|
| 3 | 9 | 2 | 1 | 6 | 4 | 7 | 5 | 8 | 2 |
| 4 | 7 | 5 | 8 | 2 | 9 | 3 | 6 | 1 | 3 |
| 8 | 6 | 1 | 7 | 9 | 5 | 2 | 3 | 4 | 4 |
| 5 | 2 | 3 | 6 | 4 | 1 | 8 | 7 | 9 | 5 |
| 7 | 4 | 9 | 2 | 3 | 8 | 6 | 1 | 5 | 6 |
| 9 | 3 | 7 | 4 | 1 | 2 | 5 | 8 | 6 | 7 |
| 2 | 8 | 6 | 9 | 5 | 7 | 1 | 4 | 3 | 8 |
| 1 | 5 | 4 | 3 | 8 | 6 | 9 | 2 | 7 | 9 |

A  B  C  D  E  F  G  H  I

# Speed Sudoku

Filling in the hard and soft clues and the listing and counting methods are traditional Sudoku solving techniques that some players use to become proficient in solving Sudoku puzzles. Now, add the dimension of speed to the solving process. The techniques in this section help in finding solutions to puzzles in the quickest way possible.

After introducing the techniques one by one, use each of them in the sample puzzles that follow. The solving tools used are virtually identical to the methods already developed, however, the order these are applied will be slightly different so that the solutions can be reached more quickly – with less time consuming drudgery. Continue to use Pointing Pairs, Pointing Triples, hidden doubles and triples, the "can be can't be" method, and analyzing the columns, rows and boxes.

To begin Speed Sudoku, work through each number, finding as many solid clues, Pointing Pairs and Pointing Triples as you can. Always start with number 1 and work up to number 9. Fill in as many cells as possible using this method. Then you go back, using the new clues to solve the rest of the puzzle in combination with the other methods already learned in this guide.

# Worksheet for Puzzle 1

Cut along the dotted line to remove the worksheet.

| | | | 1 | | | | | 4 |
|---|---|---|---|---|---|---|---|---|
| | | 1 | | | 5 | 2 | 8 | |
| | | | 7 | | 4 | 6 | | |
| | 5 | | | | 6 | 3 | | |
| 3 | 7 | | | | | | 2 | 1 |
| | 2 | | 9 | | | | 5 | |
| | | 4 | 8 | | 1 | | | |
| | 3 | 5 | 6 | | | 4 | | |
| 2 | | | | 9 | | | | |

## Puzzle 1

Follow the steps associated with each puzzle grid in this section to work a Sudoku puzzle using speed methods.

Puzzle 1  Grid 1

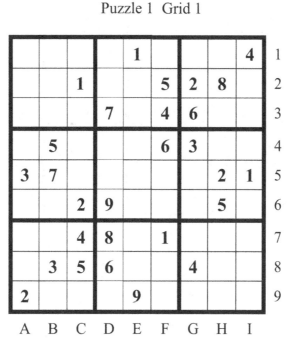

**Step 1)** Begin with the number 1 and work through the puzzle filling in *only solid clues, pointing pairs, and pointing triples. Don't fill in the soft clues unless they fall into pairs and triples.*

Puzzle 1  Grid 2

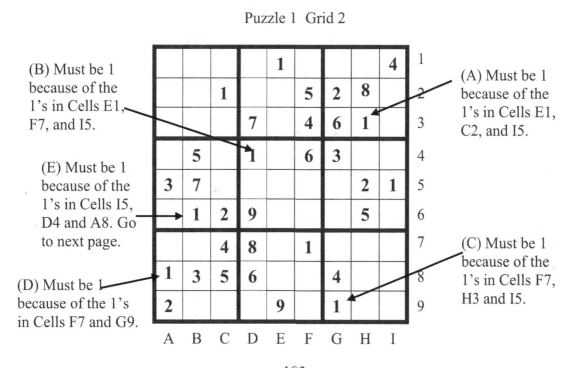

(B) Must be 1 because of the 1's in Cells E1, F7, and I5.

(E) Must be 1 because of the 1's in Cells I5, D4 and A8. Go to next page.

(D) Must be 1 because of the 1's in Cells F7 and G9.

(A) Must be 1 because of the 1's in Cells E1, C2, and I5.

(C) Must be 1 because of the 1's in Cells F7, H3 and I5.

Grid 2

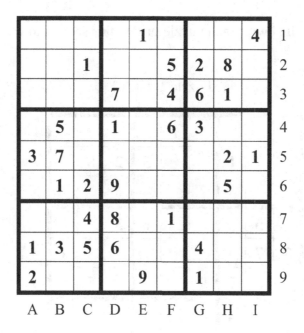

**Step 2)** Notice that some clues have been missed. Continue to rotate through the numbers 1 through 9, picking up the missing clues. Move now to number 2.

Puzzle 1  Grid 3

(G) There are no more pair or triple 3's. Move on to 4. Go to next page.

(B) Fill in soft 2's (Pointing Pair).

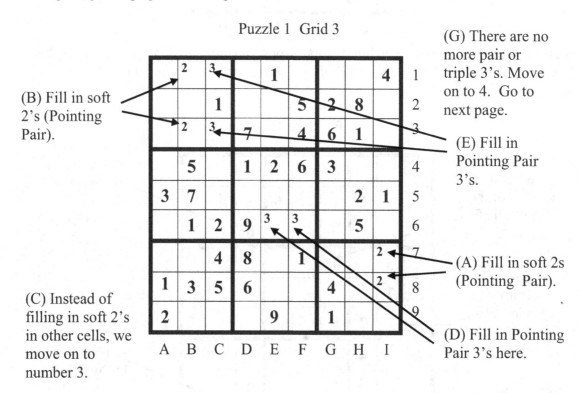

(E) Fill in Pointing Pair 3's.

(A) Fill in soft 2s (Pointing Pair).

(C) Instead of filling in soft 2's in other cells, we move on to number 3.

(D) Fill in Pointing Pair 3's here.

Grid 3

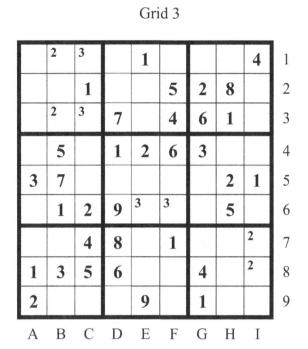

**Step 3)** Continue filling in the numbers in order, either hard clues or soft clue Pointing Pairs and Triples.

Puzzle 1  Grid 4

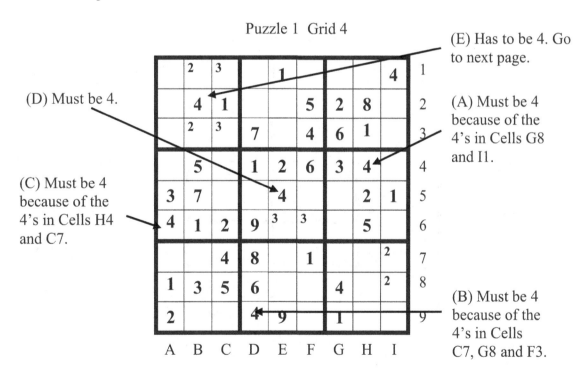

(E) Has to be 4. Go to next page.

(D) Must be 4.

(A) Must be 4 because of the 4's in Cells G8 and I1.

(C) Must be 4 because of the 4's in Cells H4 and C7.

(B) Must be 4 because of the 4's in Cells C7, G8 and F3.

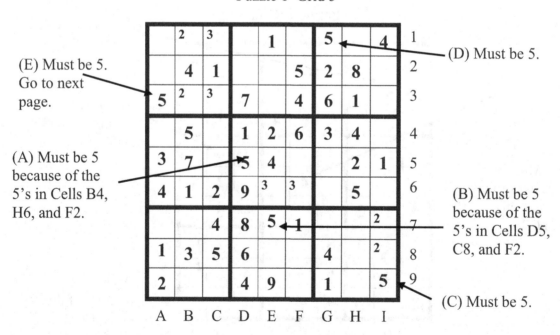

**Step 4)** Continue to the number 5.

Puzzle 1  Grid 5

(D) Must be 5.

(E) Must be 5.
Go to next
page.

(A) Must be 5
because of the
5's in Cells B4,
H6, and F2.

(B) Must be 5
because of the
5's in Cells D5,
C8, and F2.

(C) Must be 5.

Grid 5

| | A | B | C | D | E | F | G | H | I |
|---|---|---|---|---|---|---|---|---|---|
| 1 | | 2 | 3 | | 1 | | 5 | | 4 |
| 2 | | 4 | 1 | | | 5 | 2 | 8 | |
| 3 | 5 | 2 | 3 | 7 | | 4 | 6 | 1 | |
| 4 | | 5 | | 1 | 2 | 6 | 3 | 4 | |
| 5 | 3 | 7 | | 5 | 4 | | | 2 | 1 |
| 6 | 4 | 1 | 2 | 9 | 3 | 3 | | 5 | |
| 7 | | | 4 | 8 | 5 | 1 | | | 2 |
| 8 | 1 | 3 | 5 | 6 | | | 4 | | 2 |
| 9 | 2 | | | 4 | 9 | | 1 | | 5 |

**Step 5)** Continue to work the clues involving the number 6.

Puzzle 1 Grid 6

| | A | B | C | D | E | F | G | H | I |
|---|---|---|---|---|---|---|---|---|---|
| 1 | 6 | 2 6 | 3 | | 1 | | 5 | | 4 |
| 2 | | 4 | 1 | | 6 | 5 | 2 | 8 | |
| 3 | 5 | 2 | 3 | 7 | | 4 | 6 | 1 | |
| 4 | | 5 | | 1 | 2 | 6 | 3 | 4 | |
| 5 | 3 | 7 | 6 | 5 | 4 | | | 2 | 1 |
| 6 | 4 | 1 | 2 | 9 | 3 | 3 | | 5 | 6 |
| 7 | | | 4 | 8 | 5 | 1 | | 6 | 2 |
| 8 | 1 | 3 | 5 | 6 | | | 4 | | 2 |
| 9 | 2 | | | 4 | 9 | | 1 | 6 | 5 |

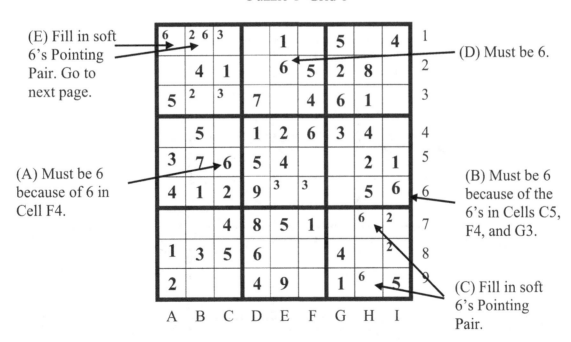

(E) Fill in soft 6's Pointing Pair. Go to next page.

(D) Must be 6.

(A) Must be 6 because of 6 in Cell F4.

(B) Must be 6 because of the 6's in Cells C5, F4, and G3.

(C) Fill in soft 6's Pointing Pair.

Grid 6

**Step 6)** Move to locate solid clues, Pointing Pairs, and Pointing Triples revolving around the number 7, see that at this point in the puzzle there are no clues to be filled in using the number 7. So, move to the number 8.

Puzzle 1  Grid 7

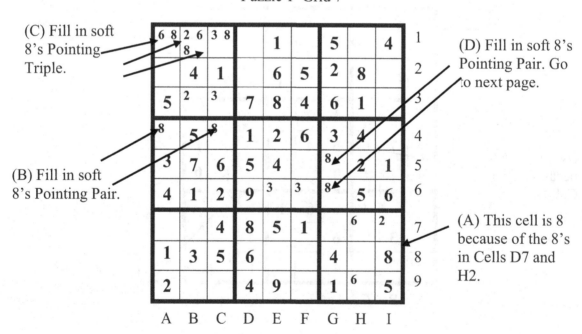

(C) Fill in soft 8's Pointing Triple.

(B) Fill in soft 8's Pointing Pair.

(D) Fill in soft 8's Pointing Pair. Go to next page.

(A) This cell is 8 because of the 8's in Cells D7 and H2.

Grid 7

Step 7) Now we continue to fill in clues associated with the number 9.

Puzzle 1 Grid 8

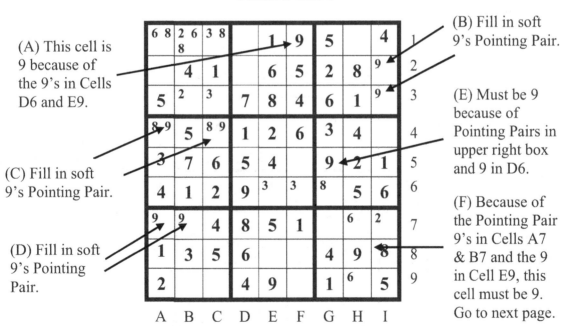

(A) This cell is 9 because of the 9's in Cells D6 and E9.

(C) Fill in soft 9's Pointing Pair.

(D) Fill in soft 9's Pointing Pair.

(B) Fill in soft 9's Pointing Pair.

(E) Must be 9 because of Pointing Pairs in upper right box and 9 in D6.

(F) Because of the Pointing Pair 9's in Cells A7 & B7 and the 9 in Cell E9, this cell must be 9. Go to next page.

| | A | B | C | D | E | F | G | H | I | |
|---|---|---|---|---|---|---|---|---|---|---|
| 1 | 6 8 | 2 6 8 | 3 8 | 1 | 9 | 5 | | 4 | | 1 |
| 2 | | 4 | 1 | 6 | 5 | 2 | 8 | (9) | | 2 |
| 3 | 5 | (2) | (3) | 7 | 8 | 4 | 6 | 1 | (9) | 3 |
| 4 | (8 9) | 5 | (8 9) | 1 | 2 | 6 | 3 | 4 | | 4 |
| 5 | 3 | 7 | 6 | 5 | 4 | | 9 | 2 | 1 | 5 |
| 6 | 4 | 1 | 2 | 9 | (3) | (3) | 8 | 5 | 6 | 6 |
| 7 | 9 | (9) | 4 | 8 | 5 | 1 | | (6) | (2) | 7 |
| 8 | 1 | 3 | 5 | 6 | | | 4 | 9 | 8 | 8 |
| 9 | 2 | | | 4 | 9 | | 1 | (6) | 5 | 9 |
| | A | B | C | D | E | F | G | H | I | |

**Step 8)** The numbers 1 through 9 have been systematically worked through, by filling in solid clues, pairs and triples. Now, check the rows, columns, and boxes for solid clues using logic and reasoning tools.

Puzzle 1  Grid 9

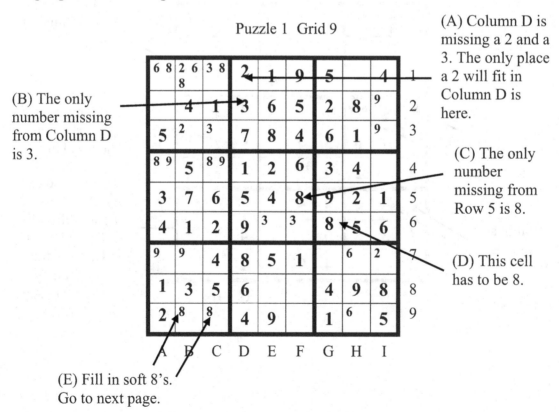

(A) Column D is missing a 2 and a 3. The only place a 2 will fit in Column D is here.

(B) The only number missing from Column D is 3.

(C) The only number missing from Row 5 is 8.

(D) This cell has to be 8.

(E) Fill in soft 8's. Go to next page.

Grid 9

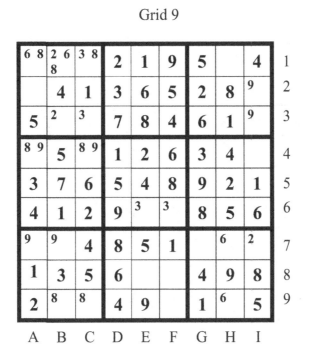

A   B   C   D   E   F   G   H   I

**Step 9)** Continue filling in solid clues until the solution is reached.

Puzzle 1  Grid 10

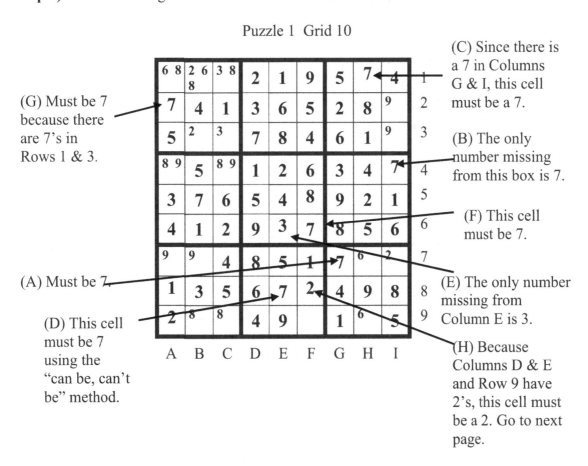

(G) Must be 7 because there are 7's in Rows 1 & 3.

(A) Must be 7.

(D) This cell must be 7 using the "can be, can't be" method.

(C) Since there is a 7 in Columns G & I, this cell must be a 7.

(B) The only number missing from this box is 7.

(F) This cell must be 7.

(E) The only number missing from Column E is 3.

(H) Because Columns D & E and Row 9 have 2's, this cell must be a 2. Go to next page.

## Grid 10

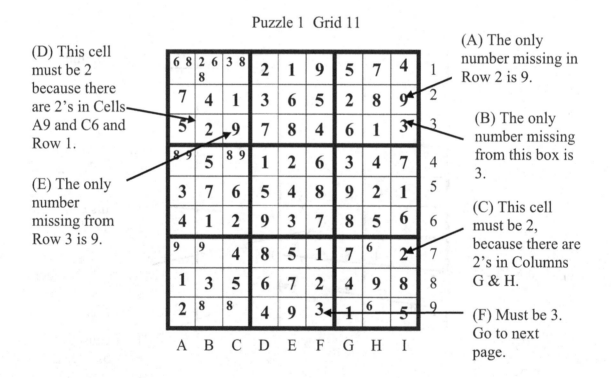

| | 6 8 | 2 6 8 | 3 8 | 2 | 1 | 9 | 5 | 7 | 4 | 1 |
| 7 | 4 | 1 | 3 | 6 | 5 | 2 | 8 | 9 | 2 |
| 5 | 2 | 3 | 7 | 8 | 4 | 6 | 1 | 9 | 3 |
| 8 9 | 5 | 8 9 | 1 | 2 | 6 | 3 | 4 | 7 | 4 |
| 3 | 7 | 6 | 5 | 4 | 8 | 9 | 2 | 1 | 5 |
| 4 | 1 | 2 | 9 | 3 | 7 | 8 | 5 | 6 | 6 |
| 9 | 9 | 4 | 8 | 5 | 1 | 7 | 6 | 2 | 7 |
| 1 | 3 | 5 | 6 | 7 | 2 | 4 | 9 | 8 | 8 |
| 2 | 8 | 8 | 4 | 9 | | 1 | 6 | 5 | 9 |

A  B  C  D  E  F  G  H  I

## Puzzle 1  Grid 11

(D) This cell must be 2 because there are 2's in Cells A9 and C6 and Row 1.

(E) The only number missing from Row 3 is 9.

(A) The only number missing in Row 2 is 9.

(B) The only number missing from this box is 3.

(C) This cell must be 2, because there are 2's in Columns G & H.

(F) Must be 3. Go to next page.

112

## Grid 11

| | | | | | | | | | |
|---|---|---|---|---|---|---|---|---|---|
| 6 8 | 2 6 8 | 3 8 | 2 | 1 | 9 | 5 | 7 | 4 | 1 |
| 7 | 4 | 1 | 3 | 6 | 5 | 2 | 8 | 9 | 2 |
| 5 | 2 | 9 | 7 | 8 | 4 | 6 | 1 | 3 | 3 |
| 8 9 | 5 | 8 9 | 1 | 2 | 6 | 3 | 4 | 7 | 4 |
| 3 | 7 | 6 | 5 | 4 | 8 | 9 | 2 | 1 | 5 |
| 4 | 1 | 2 | 9 | 3 | 7 | 8 | 5 | 6 | 6 |
| 9 | 9 | 4 | 8 | 5 | 1 | 7 | 6 | 2 | 7 |
| 1 | 3 | 5 | 6 | 7 | 2 | 4 | 9 | 8 | 8 |
| 2 | 8 | 8 | 4 | 9 | 3 | 1 | 6 | 5 | 9 |

A   B   C   D   E   F   G   H   I

## Puzzle 1  Grid 12

(A) Because there are 3's in Columns A & B, this cell must be a 3.

(C) The only number missing from Column C is 8, therefore, this cell is an 8.

(D) This cell must be 8. Go to next page.

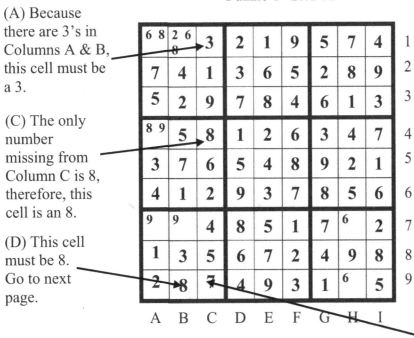

(B) Column B and Rows 7 & 8 already have 7's, so this Cell must be a 7.

## Grid 12

| | A | B | C | D | E | F | G | H | I | |
|---|---|---|---|---|---|---|---|---|---|---|
| 1 | 6 8 | 2 6 8 | 3 | 2 | 1 | 9 | 5 | 7 | 4 | 1 |
| 2 | 7 | 4 | 1 | 3 | 6 | 5 | 2 | 8 | 9 | 2 |
| 3 | 5 | 2 | 9 | 7 | 8 | 4 | 6 | 1 | 3 | 3 |
| 4 | 8 9 | 5 | 8 | 1 | 2 | 6 | 3 | 4 | 7 | 4 |
| 5 | 3 | 7 | 6 | 5 | 4 | 8 | 9 | 2 | 1 | 5 |
| 6 | 4 | 1 | 2 | 9 | 3 | 7 | 8 | 5 | 6 | 6 |
| 7 | 9 | 9 | 4 | 8 | 5 | 1 | 7 | 6 | 2 | 7 |
| 8 | 1 | 3 | 5 | 6 | 7 | 2 | 4 | 9 | 8 | 8 |
| 9 | 2 | 8 | 7 | 4 | 9 | 3 | 1 | 6 | 5 | 9 |

A   B   C   D   E   F   G   H   I

## Puzzle 1  Grid 13

(D) Because there are 8's in Cells B9 and C4, this cell is an 8.

(E) This cell must be 6.

(C) Must be 9.

(G) Must be 6. Final Solution!

(F) Must be 9.

(A) Because there are 3's in Columns G & I, this must be a 3.

(B) Must be 6.

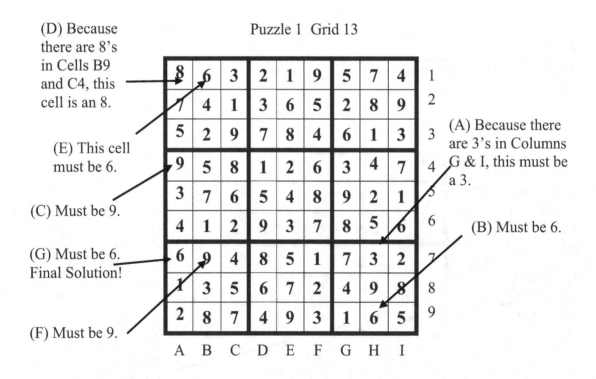

A   B   C   D   E   F   G   H   I

Puzzle 1
**Final Solution**

| | A | B | C | D | E | F | G | H | I | |
|---|---|---|---|---|---|---|---|---|---|---|
| | 8 | 6 | 3 | 2 | 1 | 9 | 5 | 7 | 4 | 1 |
| | 7 | 4 | 1 | 3 | 6 | 5 | 2 | 8 | 9 | 2 |
| | 5 | 2 | 9 | 7 | 8 | 4 | 6 | 1 | 3 | 3 |
| | 9 | 5 | 8 | 1 | 2 | 6 | 3 | 4 | 7 | 4 |
| | 3 | 7 | 6 | 5 | 4 | 8 | 9 | 2 | 1 | 5 |
| | 4 | 1 | 2 | 9 | 3 | 7 | 8 | 5 | 6 | 6 |
| | 6 | 9 | 4 | 8 | 5 | 1 | 7 | 3 | 2 | 7 |
| | 1 | 3 | 5 | 6 | 7 | 2 | 4 | 9 | 8 | 8 |
| | 2 | 8 | 7 | 4 | 9 | 3 | 1 | 6 | 5 | 9 |

## Worksheet for Puzzle 2

Cut along the dotted line to remove the worksheet.

| 6 |   | 7 | 2 |   | 8 | 3 |   | 1 |
|---|---|---|---|---|---|---|---|---|
|   | 5 |   |   |   |   |   | 4 |   |
|   |   |   | 4 |   | 6 |   |   |   |
|   |   | 4 | 9 |   | 7 | 1 |   |   |
|   |   | 9 |   |   |   | 8 |   |   |
|   |   | 8 | 1 |   | 3 | 2 |   |   |
|   |   |   | 6 |   | 5 |   |   |   |
|   | 8 |   |   |   |   |   | 2 |   |
| 9 |   | 6 | 8 |   | 2 | 5 |   | 7 |

# Puzzle 2

Puzzle 2  Grid 1

| | 6 | | 7 | 2 | | 8 | 3 | | 1 | 1 |
| | | 5 | | | | | | 4 | | 2 |
| | | | 4 | | 6 | | | | 3 |
| | | 4 | 9 | | 7 | 1 | | | 4 |
| | | 9 | | | 8 | | | 5 |
| | | 8 | 1 | | 3 | 2 | | 6 |
| | | 6 | | 5 | | | | 7 |
| | 8 | | | | | 2 | | 8 |
| 9 | | 6 | 8 | | 2 | 5 | | 7 | 9 |

A  B  C  D  E  F  G  H  I

**Step 1)** Start with the number 1, looking only for solid clues, Pointing Pairs, and Pointing Triples.

Puzzle 2  Grid 2

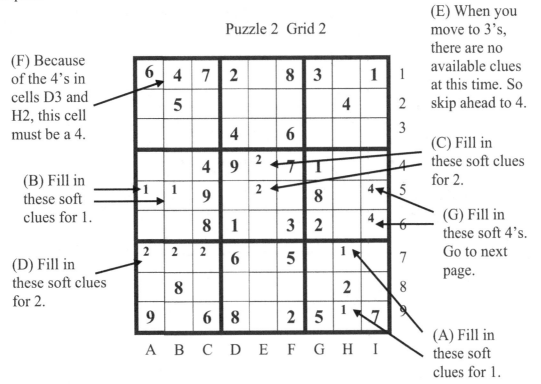

(F) Because of the 4's in cells D3 and H2, this cell must be a 4.

(B) Fill in these soft clues for 1.

(D) Fill in these soft clues for 2.

(E) When you move to 3's, there are no available clues at this time. So skip ahead to 4.

(C) Fill in these soft clues for 2.

(G) Fill in these soft 4's. Go to next page.

(A) Fill in these soft clues for 1.

119

## Grid 2

| | A | B | C | D | E | F | G | H | I | |
|---|---|---|---|---|---|---|---|---|---|---|
| 1 | 6 | 4 | 7 | 2 | | 8 | 3 | | 1 | |
| 2 | | 5 | | | | | | 4 | | |
| 3 | | | | 4 | | 6 | | | | |
| 4 | | | 4 | 9 | 2 | 7 | 1 | | | |
| 5 | 1 | 1 | 9 | | 2 | | 8 | | 4 | |
| 6 | | | 8 | 1 | | 3 | 2 | | 4 | |
| 7 | 2 | 2 | 2 | 6 | | 5 | | 1 | | |
| 8 | | 8 | | | | | | 2 | | |
| 9 | 9 | | 6 | 8 | | 2 | 5 | 1 | 7 | |

## Puzzle 2  Grid 3

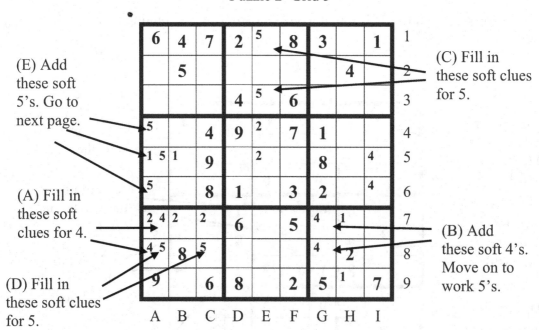

(E) Add these soft 5's. Go to next page.

(C) Fill in these soft clues for 5.

(A) Fill in these soft clues for 4.

(B) Add these soft 4's. Move on to work 5's.

(D) Fill in these soft clues for 5.

## Grid 3

| 6 | 4 | 7 | 2 | ⁵ | 8 | 3 | | 1 | 1 |
|---|---|---|---|---|---|---|---|---|---|
| | 5 | | | | | | 4 | | 2 |
| | | | 4 | ⁵ | 6 | | | | 3 |
| ⁵ | | 4 | 9 | ² | 7 | 1 | | | 4 |
| ¹ ⁵ | 1 | 9 | | ² | | | 8 | | ⁴ | 5 |
| ⁵ | | 8 | 1 | | 3 | 2 | | ⁴ | 6 |
| ² ⁴ 2 | | ² | 6 | | 5 | ⁴ | ¹ | | 7 |
| ⁴ ⁵ | 8 | ⁵ | | | | ⁴ | | 2 | 8 |
| 9 | | 6 | 8 | | 2 | 5 | ¹ | 7 | 9 |

A  B  C  D  E  F  G  H  I

## Puzzle 2  Grid 4

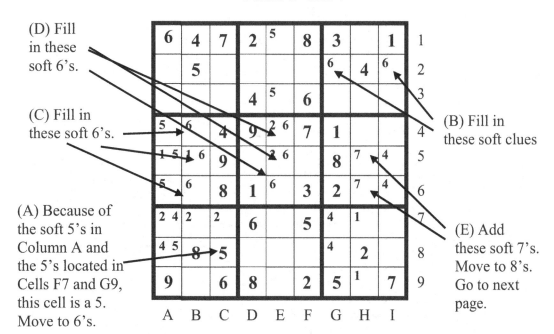

(D) Fill in these soft 6's.

(C) Fill in these soft 6's.

(A) Because of the soft 5's in Column A and the 5's located in Cells F7 and G9, this cell is a 5. Move to 6's.

(B) Fill in these soft clues

(E) Add these soft 7's. Move to 8's. Go to next page.

121

Grid 4

Puzzle 2  Grid 5

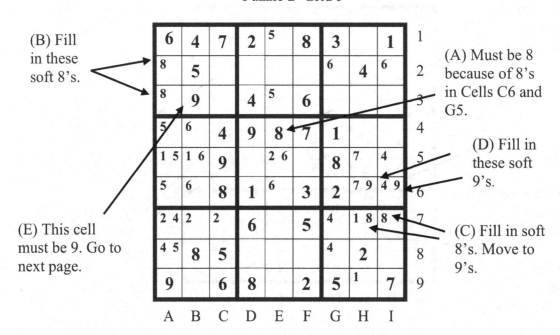

(B) Fill in these soft 8's.

(A) Must be 8 because of 8's in Cells C6 and G5.

(D) Fill in these soft 9's.

(E) This cell must be 9. Go to next page.

(C) Fill in soft 8's. Move to 9's.

## Grid 5

| | A | B | C | D | E | F | G | H | I | |
|---|---|---|---|---|---|---|---|---|---|---|
| | 6 | 4 | 7 | 2 | $^5$ | 8 | 3 | | 1 | 1 |
| | $^8$ | 5 | | | | | $^6$ | 4 | $^6$ | 2 |
| | $^8$ | 9 | | 4 | $^5$ | 6 | | | | 3 |
| | $^5$ | $^6$ | 4 | 9 | 8 | 7 | 1 | | | 4 |
| | $^{1\ 5}$ | $^{1\ 6}$ | 9 | | $^{2\ 6}$ | | 8 | $^7$ | $^4$ | 5 |
| | $^5$ | $^6$ | 8 | 1 | $^6$ | 3 | 2 | $^{7\ 9}$ | $^{4\ 9}$ | 6 |
| | $^{2\ 4}$ | $^2$ | $^2$ | 6 | | 5 | $^4$ | $^{1\ 8}$ | $^8$ | 7 |
| | $^{4\ 5}$ | 8 | 5 | | | | $^4$ | 2 | | 8 |
| | 9 | | 6 | 8 | | 2 | 5 | $^1$ | 7 | 9 |

We now analyze the rows, columns and boxes.

## Puzzle 2  Grid 6

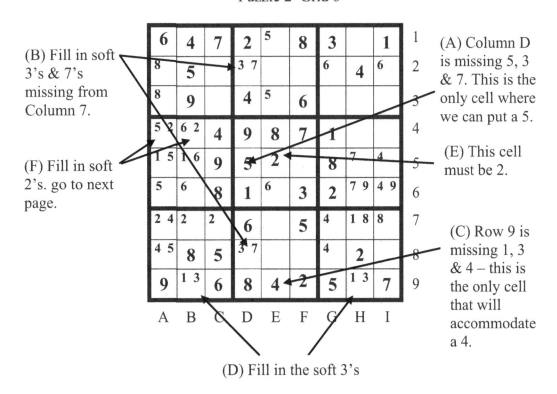

(B) Fill in soft 3's & 7's missing from Column 7.

(F) Fill in soft 2's. go to next page.

(A) Column D is missing 5, 3 & 7. This is the only cell where we can put a 5.

(E) This cell must be 2.

(C) Row 9 is missing 1, 3 & 4 – this is the only cell that will accommodate a 4.

(D) Fill in the soft 3's

123

Grid 6

|   | A | B | C | D | E | F | G | H | I |   |
|---|---|---|---|---|---|---|---|---|---|---|
| 1 | 6 | 4 | 7 | 2 ⁵ | 8 | 3 |   |   | 1 | 1 |

Grid 6 (as drawn):

Row 1: 6 | 4 | 7 | 2 (⁵) | 8 | 3 | | 1
Row 2: 8 | 5 | | 3 7 | | 6 | 4 | 6
Row 3: 8 | 9 | | 4 | ⁵ 6 | | |
Row 4: 5 2 | 6 2 | 4 | 9 | 8 | 7 | 1 | |
Row 5: 1 5 | 1 6 | 9 | 5 | 2 | | 8 | 7 | 4
Row 6: 5 | 6 | 8 | 1 | ⁶ 3 | 2 | 7 9 | 4 9
Row 7: 2 4 2 | 2 | 6 | | 5 | 4 | 1 8 | 8
Row 8: 4 5 | 8 | 5 | 3 7 | | 4 | 2 |
Row 9: 9 | 1 3 | 6 | 8 | 4 | 2 | 5 | 1 3 | 7

A  B  C  D  E  F  G  H  I

Puzzle 2  Grid 7

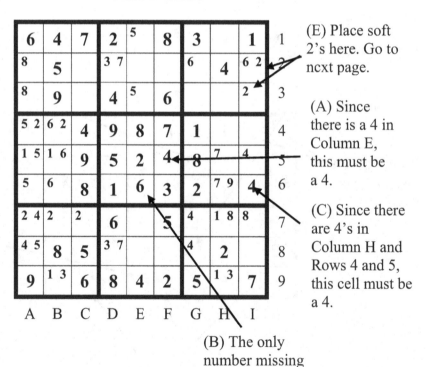

(E) Place soft 2's here. Go to ncxt page.

(A) Since there is a 4 in Column E, this must be a 4.

(D) Start working through the numbers 9 through 1 as at the beginning of the puzzle, only in descending order.

(C) Since there are 4's in Column H and Rows 4 and 5, this cell must be a 4.

(B) The only number missing from this box is 6.

# Grid 7

| | A | B | C | D | E | F | G | H | I |
|---|---|---|---|---|---|---|---|---|---|
| 1 | 6 | 4 | 7 | 2 | (5) | 8 | 3 | | 1 |
| 2 | (8) | 5 | | (3 7) | | | (6) | 4 | (6 2) |
| 3 | (8) | 9 | | 4 | (5) | 6 | | | (2) |
| 4 | (5 2) | (6 2) | 4 | 9 | 8 | 7 | 1 | | |
| 5 | (1 5) | (1 6) | 9 | 5 | 2 | 4 | 8 | (7) | (4) |
| 6 | (5) | (6) | 8 | 1 | 6 | 3 | 2 | (7 9) | 4 |
| 7 | (2 4 2) | | (2) | 6 | | 5 | (4) | (1 8) | (8) |
| 8 | (4 5) | 8 | 5 | (3 7) | | | (4) | 2 | |
| 9 | 9 | (1 3) | 6 | 8 | 4 | 2 | 5 | (1 3) | 7 |

# Puzzle 2  Grid 8

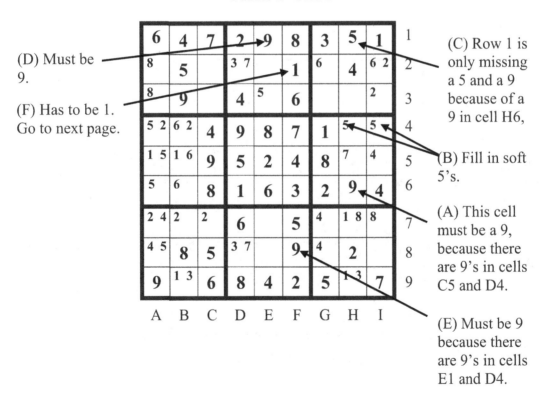

(D) Must be 9.

(F) Has to be 1. Go to next page.

(C) Row 1 is only missing a 5 and a 9 because of a 9 in cell H6,

(B) Fill in soft 5's.

(A) This cell must be a 9, because there are 9's in cells C5 and D4.

(E) Must be 9 because there are 9's in cells E1 and D4.

Grid 8

|   | A | B | C | D | E | F | G | H | I |   |
|---|---|---|---|---|---|---|---|---|---|---|
| 1 | 6 | 4 | 7 | 2 | 9 | 8 | 3 | 5 | 1 | 1 |
| 2 | 8 | 5 |   | 3 7 |   | 1 | 6 | 4 | 6 2 | 2 |
| 3 | 8 | 9 |   | 4 | 5 | 6 |   |   | 2 | 3 |
| 4 | 5 2 | 6 2 | 4 | 9 | 8 | 7 | 1 | 5 | 5 | 4 |
| 5 | 1 5 | 1 6 | 9 | 5 | 2 | 4 | 8 | 7 | 4 | 5 |
| 6 | 5 | 6 | 8 | 1 | 6 | 3 | 2 | 9 | 4 | 6 |
| 7 | 2 4 | 2 | 2 | 6 |   | 5 | 4 | 1 8 | 8 | 7 |
| 8 | 4 5 | 8 | 5 | 3 7 |   | 9 | 4 | 2 |   | 8 |
| 9 | 9 | 1 3 | 6 | 8 | 4 | 2 | 5 | 1 3 | 7 | 9 |

A  B  C  D  E  F  G  H  I

Puzzle 2  Grid 9

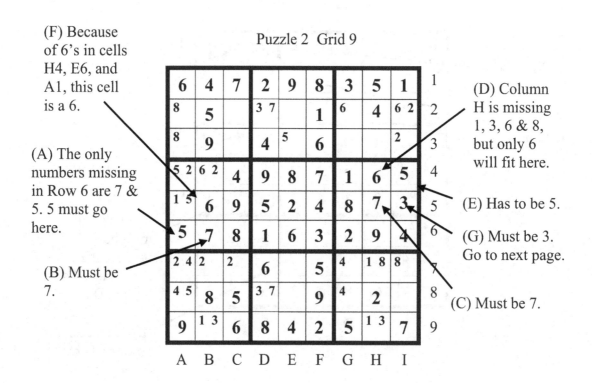

(F) Because of 6's in cells H4, E6, and A1, this cell is a 6.

(A) The only numbers missing in Row 6 are 7 & 5. 5 must go here.

(B) Must be 7.

(D) Column H is missing 1, 3, 6 & 8, but only 6 will fit here.

(E) Has to be 5.

(G) Must be 3. Go to next page.

(C) Must be 7.

126

## Grid 9

| | A | B | C | D | E | F | G | H | I | |
|---|---|---|---|---|---|---|---|---|---|---|
| 1 | 6 | 4 | 7 | 2 | 9 | 8 | 3 | 5 | 1 | 1 |
| 2 | (8) | 5 |  | (3 7) |  | 1 | (6) | 4 | (6 2) | 2 |
| 3 | (8) | 9 |  | 4 | (5) | 6 |  |  | (2) | 3 |
| 4 | (5 2) | (6 2) | 4 | 9 | 8 | 7 | 1 | 6 | 5 | 4 |
| 5 | (1 5) | 6 | 9 | 5 | 2 | 4 | 8 | 7 | 3 | 5 |
| 6 | 5 | 7 | 8 | 1 | 6 | 3 | 2 | 9 | 4 | 6 |
| 7 | (2 4) | (2) | (2) | 6 |  | 5 | (4) | 1 (8) | (8) | 7 |
| 8 | (4 5) | 8 | 5 | (3 7) |  | 9 | (4) | 2 |  | 8 |
| 9 | 9 | (1 3) | 6 | 8 | 4 | 2 | 5 | (1 3) | 7 | 9 |

A  B  C  D  E  F  G  H  I

## Puzzle 2  Grid 10

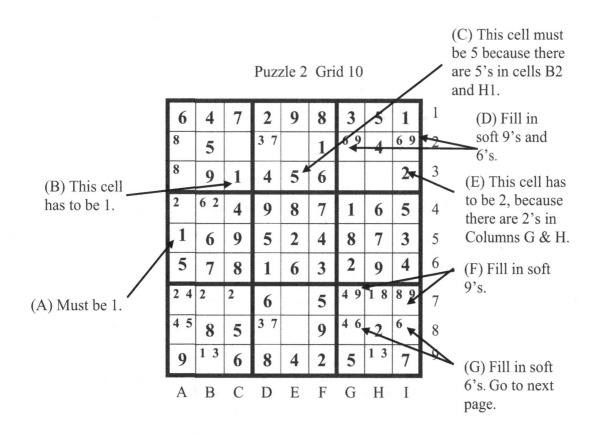

(B) This cell has to be 1.

(A) Must be 1.

(C) This cell must be 5 because there are 5's in cells B2 and H1.

(D) Fill in soft 9's and 6's.

(E) This cell has to be 2, because there are 2's in Columns G & H.

(F) Fill in soft 9's.

(G) Fill in soft 6's. Go to next page.

Grid 10

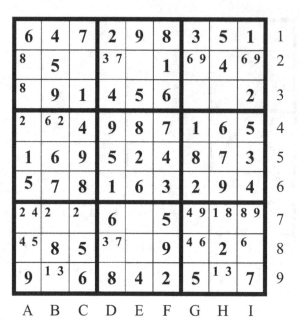

Puzzle 2  Grid 11

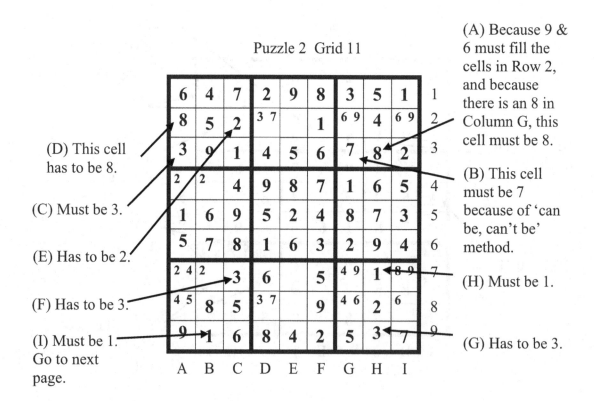

(A) Because 9 &
6 must fill the
cells in Row 2,
and because
there is an 8 in
Column G, this
cell must be 8.

(B) This cell
must be 7
because of 'can
be, can't be'
method.

(H) Must be 1.

(G) Has to be 3.

(D) This cell
has to be 8.

(C) Must be 3.

(E) Has to be 2.

(F) Has to be 3.

(I) Must be 1.
Go to next
page.

Grid 11

| | | | | | | | | | |
|---|---|---|---|---|---|---|---|---|---|
| 6 | 4 | 7 | 2 | 9 | 8 | 3 | 5 | 1 | 1 |
| 8 | 5 | 2 | 3 7 | | 1 | 6 9 | 4 | 6 9 | 2 |
| 3 | 9 | 1 | 4 | 5 | 6 | 7 | 8 | 2 | 3 |
| 2 | 2 | 4 | 9 | 8 | 7 | 1 | 6 | 5 | 4 |
| 1 | 6 | 9 | 5 | 2 | 4 | 8 | 7 | 3 | 5 |
| 5 | 7 | 8 | 1 | 6 | 3 | 2 | 9 | 4 | 6 |
| 2 4 | 2 | 3 | 6 | | 5 | 4 9 | 1 | 8 9 | 7 |
| 4 5 | 8 | 5 | 3 7 | | 9 | 4 6 | 2 | 6 | 8 |
| 9 | 1 | 6 | 8 | 4 | 2 | 5 | 3 | 7 | 9 |
| A | B | C | D | E | F | G | H | I | |

Puzzle 2 Grid 12

| | | | | | | | | | |
|---|---|---|---|---|---|---|---|---|---|
| 6 | 4 | 7 | 2 | 9 | 8 | 3 | 5 | 1 | 1 |
| 8 | 5 | 2 | 3 7 | | 1 | 6 | 4 | 9 | 2 |
| 3 | 9 | 1 | 4 | 5 | 6 | 7 | 8 | 2 | 3 |
| 2 | 3 | 4 | 9 | 8 | 7 | 1 | 6 | 5 | 4 |
| 1 | 6 | 9 | 5 | 2 | 4 | 8 | 7 | 3 | 5 |
| 5 | 7 | 8 | 1 | 6 | 3 | 2 | 9 | 4 | 6 |
| 4 | 2 | 3 | 6 | | 5 | 9 | 1 | 8 | 7 |
| 4 | 8 | 5 | 3 7 | | 9 | 4 | 2 | 6 | 8 |
| 9 | 1 | 6 | 8 | 4 | 2 | 5 | 3 | 7 | 9 |
| A | B | C | D | E | F | G | H | I | |

(A) The only numbers missing from Row 4 are 2 & 3. Because there is a 3 in A3, this cell is 3.

(B) Must be 2.

(C) Must be 8.

(D) This is the only cell in Row 7 for a 9.

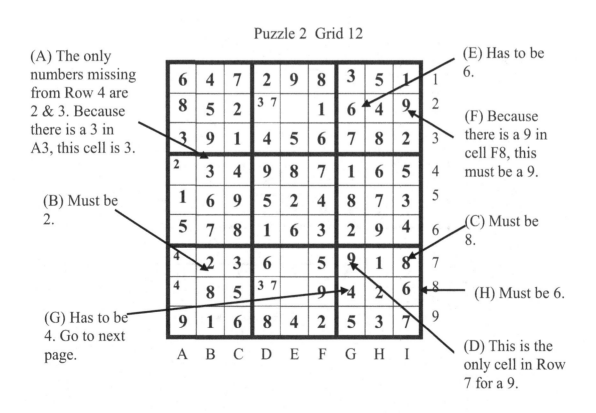

(E) Has to be 6.

(F) Because there is a 9 in cell F8, this must be a 9.

(G) Has to be 4. Go to next page.

(H) Must be 6.

## Grid 12

| | A | B | C | D | E | F | G | H | I | |
|---|---|---|---|---|---|---|---|---|---|---|
| | 6 | 4 | 7 | 2 | 9 | 8 | 3 | 5 | 1 | 1 |
| | 8 | 5 | 2 | ³ ⁷ | | 1 | 6 | 4 | 9 | 2 |
| | 3 | 9 | 1 | 4 | 5 | 6 | 7 | 8 | 2 | 3 |
| | ² | 3 | 4 | 9 | 8 | 7 | 1 | 6 | 5 | 4 |
| | 1 | 6 | 9 | 5 | 2 | 4 | 8 | 7 | 3 | 5 |
| | ⁵ | 7 | 8 | 1 | 6 | 3 | 2 | 9 | 4 | 6 |
| | ⁴ | 2 | 3 | 6 | | 5 | 9 | 1 | 8 | 7 |
| | ⁴ | 8 | 5 | ³ ⁷ | | 9 | 4 | 2 | 6 | 8 |
| | 9 | 1 | 6 | 8 | 4 | 2 | 5 | 3 | 7 | 9 |

## Puzzle 2  Grid 13

(G) Must be 7.

(C) Must be 2.

(H) Must be 3. Final Solution.

(A) Must be 4.

(D) Must be 7.

(E) Must be 1.

(B) Has to be 7.

(F) Has to be 3.

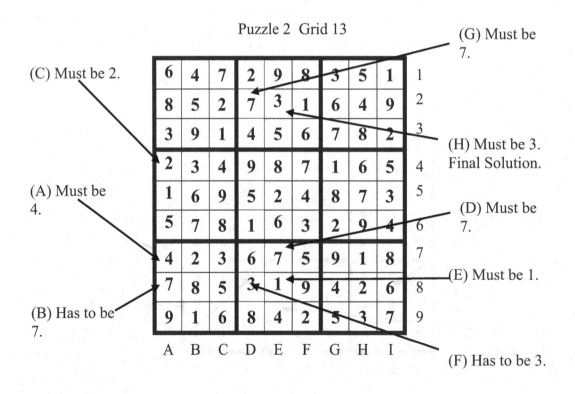

130

## Worksheet for Puzzle 3

Cut along the dotted line to remove the worksheet.

| 8 | 5 |   | 1 |   | 6 |   | 7 |   |
|---|---|---|---|---|---|---|---|---|
| 3 | 9 |   | 2 |   |   | 4 |   |   |
| 4 |   |   |   |   | 7 | 2 |   | 5 |
| 7 | 2 |   |   | 5 |   | 8 |   |   |
|   |   |   | 4 |   | 3 |   |   |   |
|   |   | 5 |   | 9 |   |   | 1 | 7 |
| 5 |   | 6 | 3 |   |   |   |   | 8 |
|   |   | 8 |   |   | 4 |   | 2 | 6 |
|   | 1 |   | 7 |   | 8 |   | 3 | 9 |

## Puzzle 3

In this example, work things differently. Instead of targeting the whole puzzle at once using the Speed Sudoku method, start working the puzzle from top left box to right bottom box. Each time work through the numbers from 1 to 9 to solve each box.

Puzzle 3

| | | | | | | | | | |
|---|---|---|---|---|---|---|---|---|---|
| 8 | 5 | | 1 | | 6 | | 7 | | 1 |
| 3 | 9 | | 2 | | | 4 | | | 2 |
| 4 | | | | 7 | 2 | | | 5 | 3 |
| 7 | 2 | | | 5 | | 8 | | | 4 |
| | | | 4 | | 3 | | | | 5 |
| | | 5 | | 9 | | | 1 | 7 | 6 |
| 5 | | 6 | 3 | | | | | 8 | 7 |
| | | 8 | | | 4 | | 2 | 6 | 8 |
| | 1 | | 7 | | 8 | | 3 | 9 | 9 |

A  B  C  D  E  F  G  H  I

Puzzle 3  Grid 1

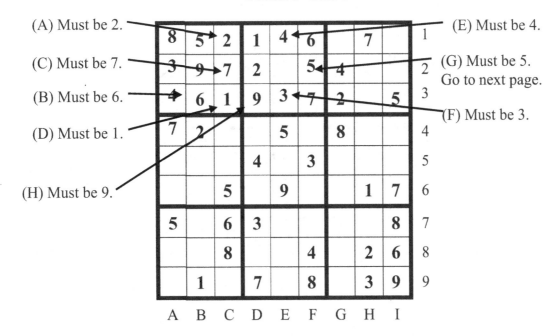

(A) Must be 2.

(C) Must be 7.

(B) Must be 6.

(D) Must be 1.

(H) Must be 9.

(E) Must be 4.

(G) Must be 5.
Go to next page.

(F) Must be 3.

133

## Grid 1

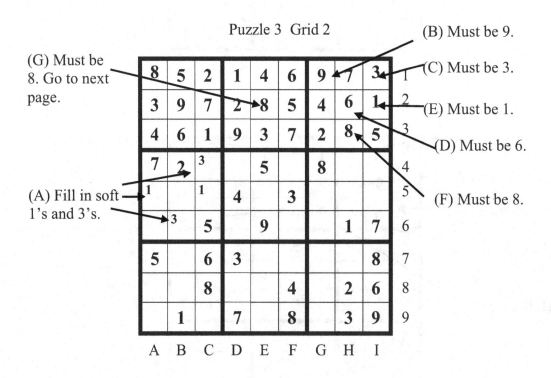

|   | A | B | C | D | E | F | G | H | I |   |
|---|---|---|---|---|---|---|---|---|---|---|
| 1 | 8 | 5 | 2 | 1 | 4 | 6 |   | 7 |   |   |
| 2 | 3 | 9 | 7 | 2 |   | 5 | 4 |   |   |   |
| 3 | 4 | 6 | 1 | 9 | 3 | 7 | 2 |   | 5 |   |
| 4 | 7 | 2 |   |   | 5 |   | 8 |   |   |   |
| 5 |   |   | 4 |   | 3 |   |   |   |   |   |
| 6 |   |   | 5 |   | 9 |   |   | 1 | 7 |   |
| 7 | 5 |   | 6 | 3 |   |   |   |   | 8 |   |
| 8 |   |   | 8 |   |   | 4 |   | 2 | 6 |   |
| 9 |   | 1 |   | 7 |   | 8 |   | 3 | 9 |   |

A  B  C  D  E  F  G  H  I

## Puzzle 3  Grid 2

(G) Must be 8. Go to next page.

(B) Must be 9.

(C) Must be 3.

(E) Must be 1.

(D) Must be 6.

(F) Must be 8.

(A) Fill in soft 1's and 3's.

A  B  C  D  E  F  G  H  I

134

## Grid 2

| | A | B | C | D | E | F | G | H | I | |
|---|---|---|---|---|---|---|---|---|---|---|
| 1 | 8 | 5 | 2 | 1 | 4 | 6 | 9 | 7 | 3 | |
| 2 | 3 | 9 | 7 | 2 | 8 | 5 | 4 | 6 | 1 | |
| 3 | 4 | 6 | 1 | 9 | 3 | 7 | 2 | 8 | 5 | |
| 4 | 7 | 2 | ³ | | 5 | | 8 | | | |
| 5 | ¹ | | ¹ | 4 | | 3 | | | | |
| 6 | | ³ | 5 | | 9 | | | 1 | 7 | |
| 7 | 5 | | 6 | 3 | | | | | 8 | |
| 8 | | | 8 | | | 4 | | 2 | 6 | |
| 9 | | 1 | | 7 | | 8 | | 3 | 9 | |

## Puzzle 3  Grid 3

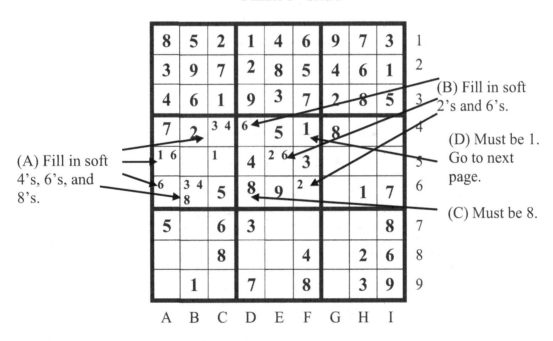

(A) Fill in soft 4's, 6's, and 8's.

(B) Fill in soft 2's and 6's.

(D) Must be 1. Go to next page.

(C) Must be 8.

Grid 3

|   |   |   |   |   |   |   |   |   |   |
|---|---|---|---|---|---|---|---|---|---|
| 8 | 5 | 2 | 1 | 4 | 6 | 9 | 7 | 3 | 1 |
| 3 | 9 | 7 | 2 | 8 | 5 | 4 | 6 | 1 | 2 |
| 4 | 6 | 1 | 9 | 3 | 7 | 2 | 8 | 5 | 3 |
| 7 | 2 | 3 4 | 6 | 5 | 1 | 8 |   |   | 4 |
| 1 6 |   | 1 | 4 | 2 6 | 3 |   |   |   | 5 |
| 6 | 3 4 8 | 5 | 8 | 9 | 2 |   | 1 | 7 | 6 |
| 5 |   | 6 | 3 |   |   |   |   | 8 | 7 |
|   |   | 8 |   |   | 4 |   | 2 | 6 | 8 |
|   | 1 |   | 7 |   | 8 |   | 3 | 9 | 9 |

A  B  C  D  E  F  G  H  I

Puzzle 3   Grid 4

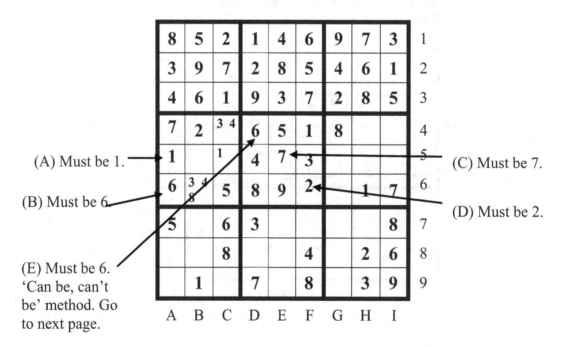

(A) Must be 1.

(B) Must be 6.

(C) Must be 7.

(D) Must be 2.

(E) Must be 6. 'Can be, can't be' method. Go to next page.

## Grid 4

| | A | B | C | D | E | F | G | H | I | |
|---|---|---|---|---|---|---|---|---|---|---|
| | 8 | 5 | 2 | 1 | 4 | 6 | 9 | 7 | 3 | 1 |
| | 3 | 9 | 7 | 2 | 8 | 5 | 4 | 6 | 1 | 2 |
| | 4 | 6 | 1 | 9 | 3 | 7 | 2 | 8 | 5 | 3 |
| | 7 | 2 | 3 4 | 6 | 5 | 1 | 8 | | | 4 |
| | 1 | | | 4 | 7 | 3 | | | | 5 |
| | 6 | 3 4 8 | 5 | 8 | 9 | 2 | | 1 | 7 | 6 |
| | 5 | | 6 | 3 | | | | | 8 | 7 |
| | | | 8 | | | 4 | | 2 | 6 | 8 |
| | | 1 | | 7 | | 8 | | 3 | 9 | 9 |

A B C D E F G H I

## Puzzle 3  Grid 5

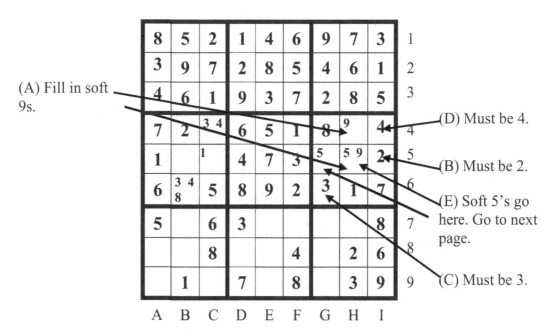

(A) Fill in soft 9s.

(D) Must be 4.

(B) Must be 2.

(E) Soft 5's go here. Go to next page.

(C) Must be 3.

Grid 5

| 8 | 5 | 2 | 1 | 4 | 6 | 9 | 7 | 3 | 1 |
| 3 | 9 | 7 | 2 | 8 | 5 | 4 | 6 | 1 | 2 |
| 4 | 6 | 1 | 9 | 3 | 7 | 2 | 8 | 5 | 3 |
| 7 | 2 | ³ ⁴ | 6 | 5 | 1 | 8 | ⁹ | 4 | 4 |
| 1 |  |  | 4 | 7 | 3 | ⁵ | ⁵ | 2 | 5 |
| 6 | ³ ⁴ ₈ | 5 | 8 | 9 | 2 | 3 | 1 | 7 | 6 |
| 5 |  | 6 | 3 |  |  |  |  | 8 | 7 |
|  |  | 8 |  |  | 4 |  | 2 | 6 | 8 |
|  | 1 |  | 7 |  | 8 |  | 3 | 9 | 9 |

A  B  C  D  E  F  G  H  I

Puzzle 3  Grid 6

(D) This cell is a 9. Go to next page.

(C) This cell must be a 9.

(B) This cell is a 5.

(A) Must be 6.

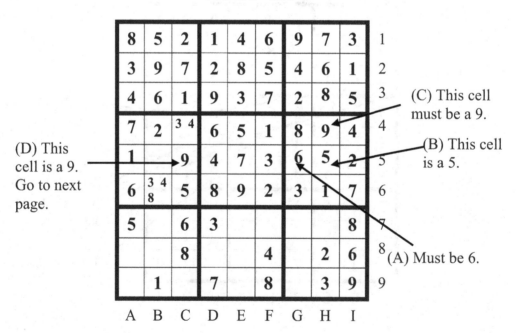

A  B  C  D  E  F  G  H  I

## Grid 6

| | A | B | C | D | E | F | G | H | I | |
|---|---|---|---|---|---|---|---|---|---|---|
| 1 | 8 | 5 | 2 | 1 | 4 | 6 | 9 | 7 | 3 | 1 |
| 2 | 3 | 9 | 7 | 2 | 8 | 5 | 4 | 6 | 1 | 2 |
| 3 | 4 | 6 | 1 | 9 | 3 | 7 | 2 | 8 | 5 | 3 |
| 4 | 7 | 2 | 3 4 | 6 | 5 | 1 | 8 | 9 | 4 | 4 |
| 5 | 1 | | 9 | 4 | 7 | 3 | 6 | 5 | 2 | 5 |
| 6 | 6 | 3 4 8 | 5 | 8 | 9 | 2 | 3 | 1 | 7 | 6 |
| 7 | 5 | | 6 | 3 | | | | | 8 | 7 |
| 8 | | | 8 | | | 4 | | 2 | 6 | 8 |
| 9 | | 1 | | 7 | | 8 | | 3 | 9 | 9 |

A  B  C  D  E  F  G  H  I

## Puzzle 3  Grid 7

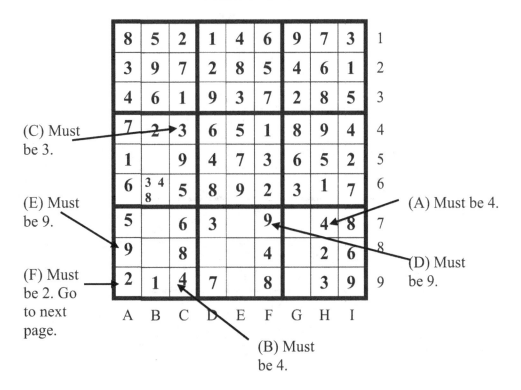

(C) Must be 3.

(E) Must be 9.

(F) Must be 2. Go to next page.

(A) Must be 4.

(D) Must be 9.

(B) Must be 4.

139

## Grid 7

| | A | B | C | D | E | F | G | H | I | |
|---|---|---|---|---|---|---|---|---|---|---|
| 1 | 8 | 5 | 2 | 1 | 4 | 6 | 9 | 7 | 3 | 1 |
| 2 | 3 | 9 | 7 | 2 | 8 | 5 | 4 | 6 | 1 | 2 |
| 3 | 4 | 6 | 1 | 9 | 3 | 7 | 2 | 8 | 5 | 3 |
| 4 | 7 | 2 | 3 | 6 | 5 | 1 | 8 | 9 | 4 | 4 |
| 5 | 1 |  | 9 | 4 | 7 | 3 | 6 | 5 | 2 | 5 |
| 6 | 6 | 3 4 8 | 5 | 8 | 9 | 2 | 3 | 1 | 7 | 6 |
| 7 | 5 |  | 6 | 3 |  | 9 |  | 4 | 8 | 7 |
| 8 | 9 |  | 8 |  |  | 4 |  | 2 | 6 | 8 |
| 9 | 2 | 1 | 4 | 7 |  | 8 |  | 3 | 9 | 9 |

A  B  C  D  E  F  G  H  I

## Puzzle 3  Grid 8

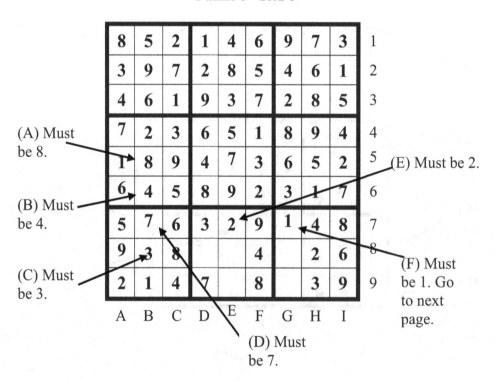

(A) Must be 8.

(B) Must be 4.

(C) Must be 3.

(D) Must be 7.

(E) Must be 2.

(F) Must be 1. Go to next page.

## Grid 8

| 8 | 5 | 2 | 1 | 4 | 6 | 9 | 7 | 3 | 1 |
|---|---|---|---|---|---|---|---|---|---|
| 3 | 9 | 7 | 2 | 8 | 5 | 4 | 6 | 1 | 2 |
| 4 | 6 | 1 | 9 | 3 | 7 | 2 | 8 | 5 | 3 |
| 7 | 2 | 3 | 6 | 5 | 1 | 8 | 9 | 4 | 4 |
| 1 | 8 | 9 | 4 | 7 | 3 | 6 | 5 | 2 | 5 |
| 6 | 4 | 5 | 8 | 9 | 2 | 3 | 1 | 7 | 6 |
| 5 | 7 | 6 | 3 | 2 | 9 | 1 | 4 | 8 | 7 |
| 9 | 3 | 8 |   |   | 4 |   | 2 | 6 | 8 |
| 2 | 1 | 4 | 7 |   | 8 |   | 3 | 9 | 9 |

A B C D E F G H I

## Puzzle 3  Grid 9
### Final Solution

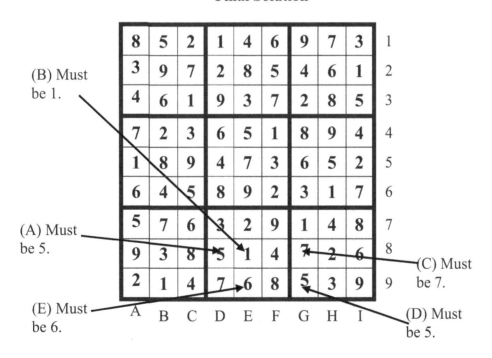

(B) Must be 1.

(A) Must be 5.

(E) Must be 6.

(C) Must be 7.

(D) Must be 5.

141

## Worksheet for Puzzle 4

Cut along the dotted line to remove the worksheet.

| | | 2 | | | | 8 | | 3 |
|---|---|---|---|---|---|---|---|---|
| | | 6 | | | 2 | | | 5 |
| 3 | | | | 9 | | | 4 | |
| | 4 | 1 | 5 | 6 | | | 8 | |
| | | | | | | | | |
| | 6 | | | 1 | 4 | 5 | 3 | |
| | 3 | | | 5 | | | | 8 |
| 9 | | | 6 | | | 3 | | |
| 2 | | 8 | | | | 7 | | |

## *Puzzle 4*

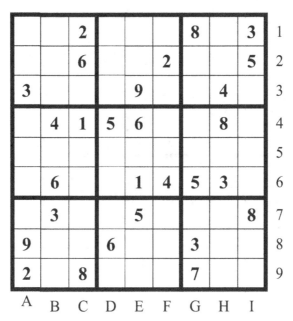

Puzzle 4  Grid 1

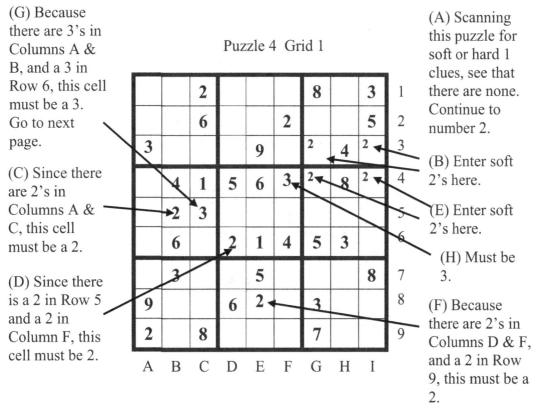

(G) Because there are 3's in Columns A & B, and a 3 in Row 6, this cell must be a 3. Go to next page.

(C) Since there are 2's in Columns A & C, this cell must be a 2.

(D) Since there is a 2 in Row 5 and a 2 in Column F, this cell must be 2.

(A) Scanning this puzzle for soft or hard 1 clues, see that there are none. Continue to number 2.

(B) Enter soft 2's here.

(E) Enter soft 2's here.

(H) Must be 3.

(F) Because there are 2's in Columns D & F, and a 2 in Row 9, this must be a 2.

Grid 1

| | A | B | C | D | E | F | G | H | I | |
|---|---|---|---|---|---|---|---|---|---|---|
| 1 | | | 2 | | | | 8 | | 3 | 1 |
| 2 | | | 6 | | | 2 | | | 5 | 2 |
| 3 | 3 | | | | 9 | | 2 | 4 | 2 | 3 |
| 4 | | 4 | 1 | 5 | 6 | 3 | 2 | 8 | 2 | 4 |
| 5 | | 2 | 3 | | | | | | | 5 |
| 6 | | 6 | | 2 | 1 | 4 | 5 | 3 | | 6 |
| 7 | | 3 | | | 5 | | | | 8 | 7 |
| 8 | 9 | | | 6 | 2 | | 3 | | | 8 |
| 9 | 2 | | 8 | | | | 7 | | | 9 |

Puzzle 4  Grid 2

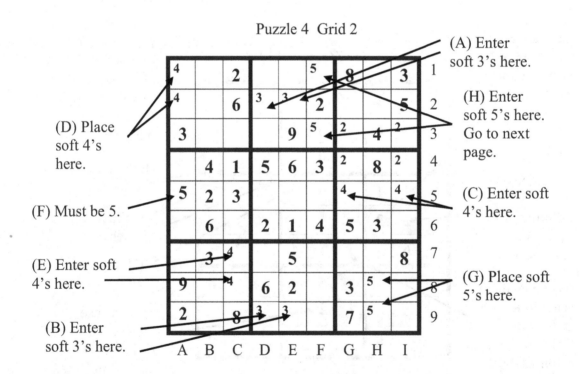

(A) Enter soft 3's here.

(H) Enter soft 5's here. Go to next page.

(D) Place soft 4's here.

(C) Enter soft 4's here.

(F) Must be 5.

(E) Enter soft 4's here.

(G) Place soft 5's here.

(B) Enter soft 3's here.

146

Grid 2

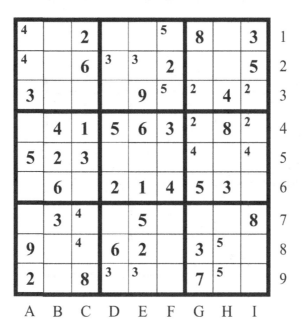

A   B   C   D   E   F   G   H   I

Puzzle 4  Grid 3

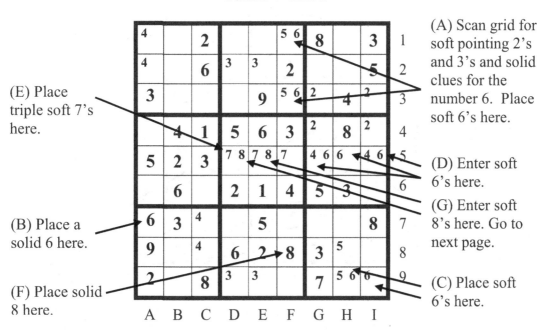

(A) Scan grid for soft pointing 2's and 3's and solid clues for the number 6. Place soft 6's here.

(E) Place triple soft 7's here.

(D) Enter soft 6's here.

(G) Enter soft 8's here. Go to next page.

(B) Place a solid 6 here.

(F) Place solid 8 here.

(C) Place soft 6's here.

147

# Grid 3

A  B  C  D  E  F  G  H  I

Puzzle 4  Grid 4

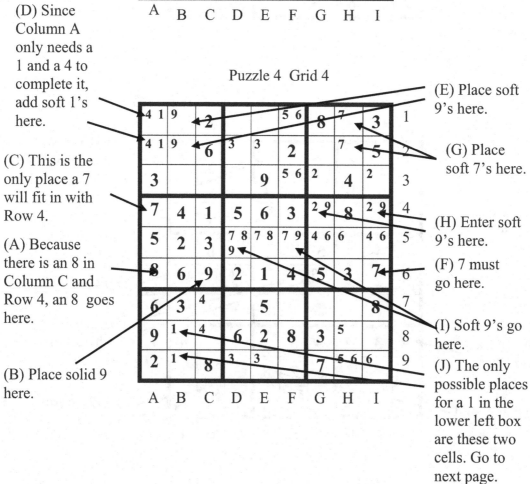

(D) Since Column A only needs a 1 and a 4 to complete it, add soft 1's here.

(C) This is the only place a 7 will fit in with Row 4.

(A) Because there is an 8 in Column C and Row 4, an 8 goes here.

(B) Place solid 9 here.

(E) Place soft 9's here.

(G) Place soft 7's here.

(H) Enter soft 9's here.

(F) 7 must go here.

(I) Soft 9's go here.

(J) The only possible places for a 1 in the lower left box are these two cells. Go to next page.

A  B  C  D  E  F  G  H  I

148

## Grid 4

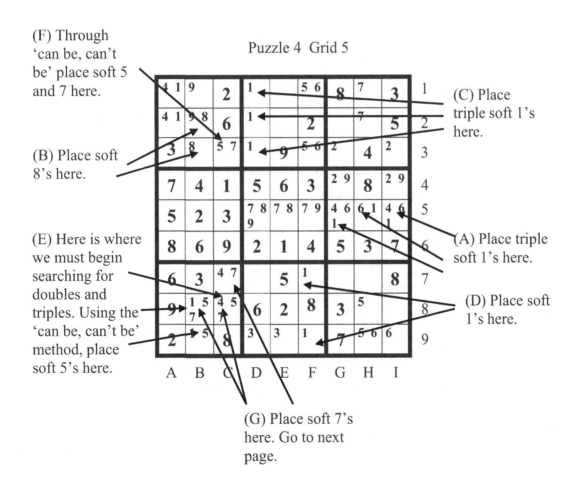

|   | A | B | C | D | E | F | G | H | I |   |
|---|---|---|---|---|---|---|---|---|---|---|
| 1 | 4 1 9 |   | 2 |   |   | 5 6 | 8 | 7 | 3 | 1 |
| 2 | 4 1 9 |   | 6 | 3 | 3 | 2 |   | 7 | 5 | 2 |
| 3 | 3 |   |   |   | 9 | 5 6 2 | 2 | 4 | 2 | 3 |
| 4 | 7 | 4 | 1 | 5 | 6 | 3 | 2 9 | 8 | 2 9 | 4 |
| 5 | 5 | 2 | 3 | 7 8 9 | 7 8 | 7 9 | 4 6 6 | 6 | 4 6 | 5 |
| 6 | 8 | 6 | 9 | 2 | 1 | 4 | 5 | 3 | 7 | 6 |
| 7 | 6 | 3 | 4 |   | 5 |   |   |   | 8 | 7 |
| 8 | 9 | 1 | 4 | 6 | 2 | 8 | 3 | 5 |   | 8 |
| 9 | 2 | 1 | 8 | 3 | 3 |   | 7 | 5 6 6 |   | 9 |

(F) Through 'can be, can't be' place soft 5 and 7 here.

(B) Place soft 8's here.

(E) Here is where we must begin searching for doubles and triples. Using the 'can be, can't be' method, place soft 5's here.

## Puzzle 4  Grid 5

(C) Place triple soft 1's here.

(A) Place triple soft 1's here.

(D) Place soft 1's here.

(G) Place soft 7's here. Go to next page.

149

## Grid 5

| | A | B | C | D | E | F | G | H | I | |
|---|---|---|---|---|---|---|---|---|---|---|
| **1** | 4 1 9 **2** | | | **1** | | 5 6 | **8** | **7** | **3** | 1 |
| **2** | 4 1 9 8 **6** | | | **1** | | **2** | | **7** | **5** | 2 |
| **3** | **3** | 8 | 5 7 | **1** | **9** | 5 6 | **2** | **4** | **2** | 3 |
| **4** | **7** | **4** | **1** | **5** | **6** | **3** | 2 9 **8** | | 2 9 | 4 |
| **5** | **5** | **2** | **3** | 7 8 9 | 7 8 | 7 9 | 4 6 1 | 6 1 | 4 6 1 | 5 |
| **6** | **8** | **6** | **9** | **2** | **1** | **4** | **5** | **3** | **7** | 6 |
| **7** | **6** | **3** | 4 7 | | **5** | 1 | | | **8** | 7 |
| **8** | **9** | 1 5 7 | 4 5 7 | **6** | **2** | **8** | **3** | 5 | | 8 |
| **9** | **2** | 1 5 | **8** | 3 | 3 | 1 | **7** | 5 6 | 6 | 9 |

A  B  C  D  E  F  G  H  I

## Puzzle 4  Grid 6

(A) Using 'can be, can't be' fill in soft clues..

(B) Using an advanced technique derived from the "Creating Your Own Sudoku" paradigm, this cell must be a 4 because it's the only number that can be paired with the 3 in cell C7.

(D) Must be 4. Go to next page.

(C) Must be 4.

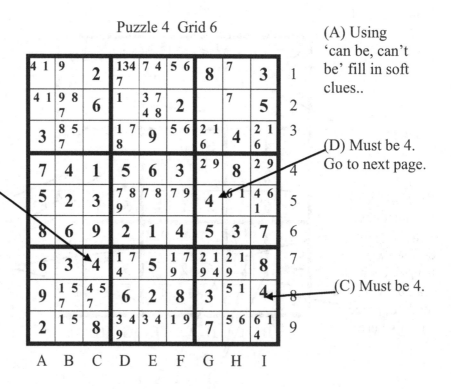

Grid 6

Puzzle 4  Grid 7

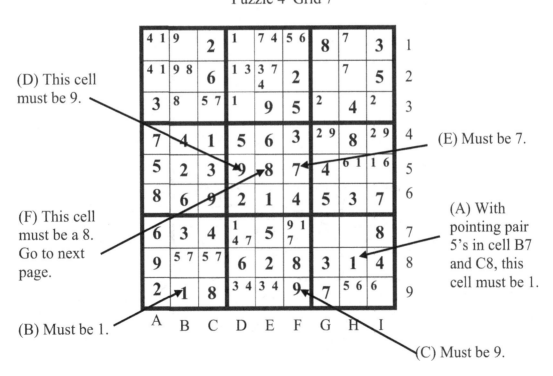

(D) This cell must be 9.

(E) Must be 7.

(F) This cell must be a 8. Go to next page.

(A) With pointing pair 5's in cell B7 and C8, this cell must be 1.

(B) Must be 1.

(C) Must be 9.

151

Grid 7

Puzzle 4  Grid 8

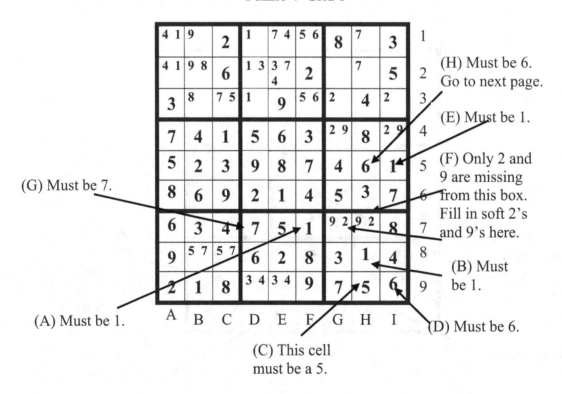

(H) Must be 6.
Go to next page.

(E) Must be 1.

(F) Only 2 and
9 are missing
from this box.
Fill in soft 2's
and 9's here.

(G) Must be 7.

(B) Must
be 1.

(A) Must be 1.

(D) Must be 6.

(C) This cell
must be a 5.

Grid 8

| | A | B | C | D | E | F | G | H | I | |
|---|---|---|---|---|---|---|---|---|---|---|
| 1 | 4 1 9 / **2** | | | 1 / 7 4 / 5 6 | | | **8** | 7 | **3** | 1 |
| 2 | 4 1 9 8 / **6** | | | 1 3 / 3 7 4 | **2** | | | 7 | **5** | 2 |
| 3 | **3** | 8 | 5 7 | 1 / **9** | | 5 6 | 2 / **4** | | 2 | 3 |
| 4 | **7** | **4** | **1** | **5** | **6** | **3** | 2 9 / **8** | | 2 9 | 4 |
| 5 | **5** | **2** | **3** | **9** | **8** | **7** | **4** | **6** | **1** | 5 |
| 6 | **8** | **6** | **9** | **2** | **1** | **4** | **5** | **3** | **7** | 6 |
| 7 | **6** | **3** | **4** | **7** | **5** | **1** | 2 9 | 2 9 / **8** | | 7 |
| 8 | **9** | 5 7 | 5 7 | **6** | **2** | **8** | **3** | **1** | **4** | 8 |
| 9 | **2** | **1** | **8** | 3 4 | 3 4 / **9** | | **7** | **5** | **6** | 9 |

Puzzle 4  Grid 9

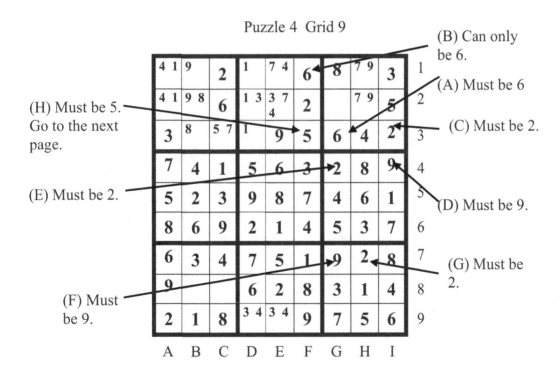

(B) Can only be 6.

(A) Must be 6

(C) Must be 2.

(H) Must be 5. Go to the next page.

(E) Must be 2.

(D) Must be 9.

(G) Must be 2.

(F) Must be 9.

## Grid 9

| | A | B | C | D | E | F | G | H | I | |
|---|---|---|---|---|---|---|---|---|---|---|
| 1 | (4 1 9) | | **2** | (1 · 7 4) | | **6** | **8** | (7 9) | **3** | 1 |
| 2 | (4 1 · 9 8) | | **6** | (1 3 · 3 7 4) | **2** | | | (7 9) | **5** | 2 |
| 3 | **3** | (8) | (5 7) | (1) | **9** | **5** | **6** | **4** | **2** | 3 |
| 4 | **7** | **4** | **1** | **5** | **6** | **3** | **2** | **8** | **9** | 4 |
| 5 | **5** | **2** | **3** | **9** | **8** | **7** | **4** | **6** | **1** | 5 |
| 6 | **8** | **6** | **9** | **2** | **1** | **4** | **5** | **3** | **7** | 6 |
| 7 | **6** | **3** | **4** | **7** | **5** | **1** | **9** | **2** | **8** | 7 |
| 8 | **9** | | | **6** | **2** | **8** | **3** | **1** | **4** | 8 |
| 9 | **2** | **1** | **8** | (3 4) | (3 4) | **9** | **7** | **5** | **6** | 9 |

A  B  C  D  E  F  G  H  I

Puzzle 4  Grid 10

(E) Fill in soft 8's in Cells D2 and E2.

(C) Must be 1.

(I) Must be 5. Go to next page.

(B) Must be 4.

(F) Must be 8.

(G) Must be 7.

(A) Must be 1.

(H) Must be 9.

(D) Must be 1.

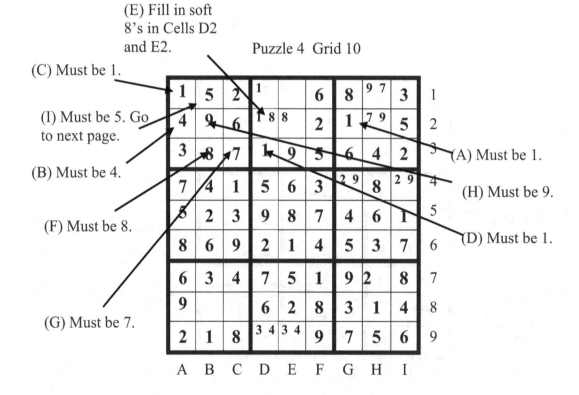

| | A | B | C | D | E | F | G | H | I | |
|---|---|---|---|---|---|---|---|---|---|---|
| 1 | **1** | **5** | **2** | (1) | | **6** | **8** | (9 7) | **3** | 1 |
| 2 | **4** | **9** | **6** | (1 · 8 8) | | **2** | **1** | (7 9) | **5** | 2 |
| 3 | **3** | **8** | **7** | (1) | **9** | **5** | **6** | **4** | **2** | 3 |
| 4 | **7** | **4** | **1** | **5** | **6** | **3** | (2 9) | **8** | (2 9) | 4 |
| 5 | **5** | **2** | **3** | **9** | **8** | **7** | **4** | **6** | **1** | 5 |
| 6 | **8** | **6** | **9** | **2** | **1** | **4** | **5** | **3** | **7** | 6 |
| 7 | **6** | **3** | **4** | **7** | **5** | **1** | **9** | **2** | **8** | 7 |
| 8 | **9** | | | **6** | **2** | **8** | **3** | **1** | **4** | 8 |
| 9 | **2** | **1** | **8** | (3 4) | (3 4) | **9** | **7** | **5** | **6** | 9 |

A  B  C  D  E  F  G  H  I

154

# Grid 10

| | A | B | C | D | E | F | G | H | I | |
|---|---|---|---|---|---|---|---|---|---|---|
| 1 | 1 | 5 | 2 | ¹ | | 6 | 8 | ⁹⁷ | 3 | 1 |
| 2 | 4 | 9 | 6 | ¹⁸ ⁸ | | 2 | 1 | ⁷⁹ | 5 | 2 |
| 3 | 3 | 8 | 7 | 1 | 9 | 5 | 6 | 4 | 2 | 3 |
| 4 | 7 | 4 | 1 | 5 | 6 | 3 | ²⁹ | 8 | ²⁹ | 4 |
| 5 | 5 | 2 | 3 | 9 | 8 | 7 | 4 | 6 | 1 | 5 |
| 6 | 8 | 6 | 9 | 2 | 1 | 4 | 5 | 3 | 7 | 6 |
| 7 | 6 | 3 | 4 | 7 | 5 | 1 | 9 | 2 | 8 | 7 |
| 8 | 9 | | | 6 | 2 | 8 | 3 | 1 | 4 | 8 |
| 9 | 2 | 1 | 8 | ³⁴ | ³⁴ | 9 | 7 | 5 | 6 | 9 |

## Puzzle 4  Grid 11
### Final Solution

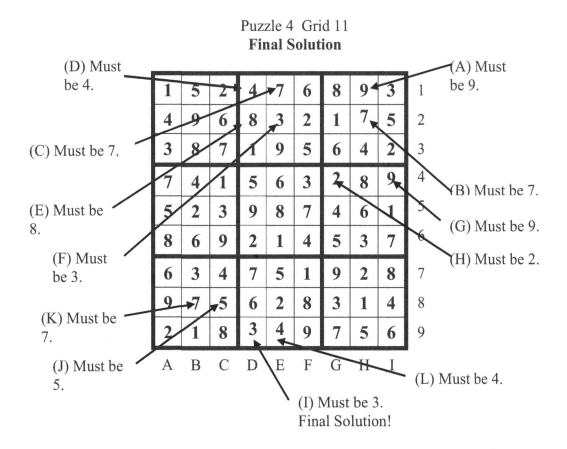

(D) Must be 4.

(A) Must be 9.

(C) Must be 7.

(E) Must be 8.

(B) Must be 7.

(F) Must be 3.

(G) Must be 9.

(H) Must be 2.

(K) Must be 7.

(J) Must be 5.

(L) Must be 4.

(I) Must be 3. Final Solution!

## Worksheet for Puzzle 5

Cut along the dotted line to remove the worksheet.

| | 4 | | | | | | 2 | |
|---|---|---|---|---|---|---|---|---|
| 1 | | | 3 | | 6 | | | 5 |
| | | 7 | 2 | 8 | 5 | 1 | | |
| 7 | | | | 6 | | | | 9 |
| | 3 | | | | | | 1 | |
| 6 | | | | 3 | | | | 4 |
| | | 2 | 1 | 9 | 3 | 5 | | |
| 8 | 1 | | 6 | | 7 | | | 2 |
| | 7 | | | | | | 6 | |

## Puzzle 5

| | A | B | C | D | E | F | G | H | I | |
|---|---|---|---|---|---|---|---|---|---|---|
| | | 4 | | | | | | 2 | | 1 |
| | 1 | | | 3 | | 6 | | | 5 | 2 |
| | | | 7 | 2 | 8 | 5 | 1 | | | 3 |
| | 7 | | | | 6 | | | | 9 | 4 |
| | | 3 | | | | | | 1 | | 5 |
| | 6 | | | | 3 | | | | 4 | 6 |
| | | | 2 | 1 | 9 | 3 | 5 | | | 7 |
| | 8 | 1 | | 6 | | 7 | | | 2 | 8 |
| | | 7 | | | | | | 6 | | 9 |

Puzzle 5 Grid 1

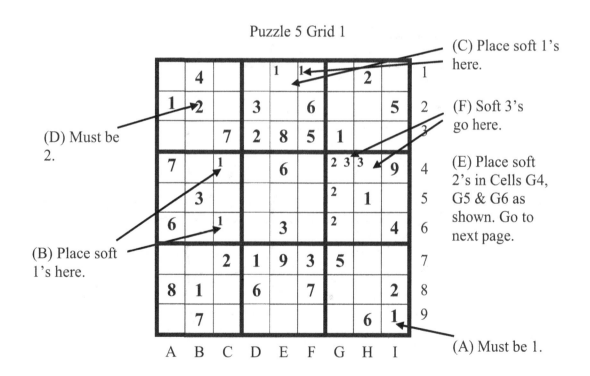

(C) Place soft 1's here.

(D) Must be 2.

(F) Soft 3's go here.

(E) Place soft 2's in Cells G4, G5 & G6 as shown. Go to next page.

(B) Place soft 1's here.

(A) Must be 1.

Grid 1

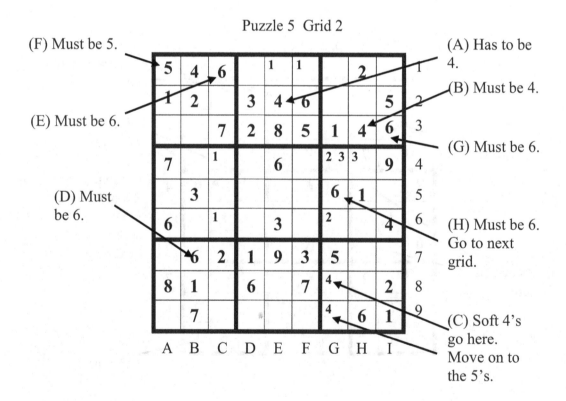

Puzzle 5  Grid 2

(F) Must be 5.

(E) Must be 6.

(D) Must be 6.

(A) Has to be 4.

(B) Must be 4.

(G) Must be 6.

(H) Must be 6. Go to next grid.

(C) Soft 4's go here. Move on to the 5's.

Grid 2

| | A | B | C | D | E | F | G | H | I | |
|---|---|---|---|---|---|---|---|---|---|---|
| 1 | 5 | 4 | 6 | ¹ | ¹ | | | 2 | | 1 |
| 2 | 1 | 2 | | 3 | 4 | 6 | | | 5 | 2 |
| 3 | | | 7 | 2 | 8 | 5 | 1 | 4 | 6 | 3 |
| 4 | 7 | | ¹ | | 6 | | ²³ ³ | | 9 | 4 |
| 5 | | 3 | | | | | 6 | 1 | | 5 |
| 6 | 6 | | ¹ | | 3 | | ² | | 4 | 6 |
| 7 | | 6 | 2 | 1 | 9 | 3 | 5 | | | 7 |
| 8 | 8 | 1 | | | 6 | | ⁴ | | 2 | 8 |
| 9 | | 7 | | | | | ⁴ | 6 | 1 | 9 |

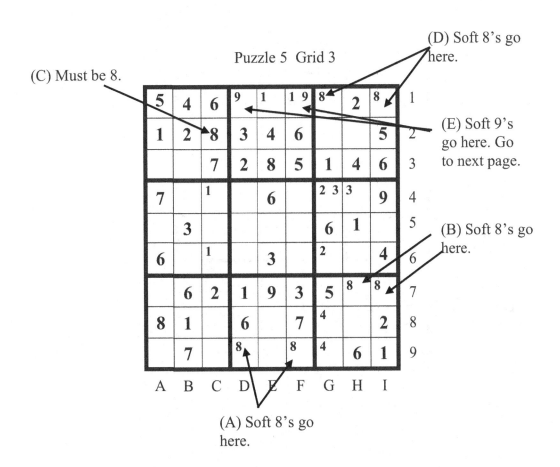

(C) Must be 8.

(D) Soft 8's go here.

Puzzle 5  Grid 3

(E) Soft 9's go here. Go to next page.

(B) Soft 8's go here.

(A) Soft 8's go here.

161

**Grid 3**

| | A | B | C | D | E | F | G | H | I | |
|---|---|---|---|---|---|---|---|---|---|---|
| 1 | 5 | 4 | 6 | 9 | 1 | 1 9 | 8 | 2 | 8 | 1 |
| 2 | 1 | 2 | 8 | 3 | 4 | 6 | | | 5 | 2 |
| 3 | | | 7 | 2 | 8 | 5 | 1 | 4 | 6 | 3 |
| 4 | 7 | 1 | | | 6 | | 2 3 3 | | 9 | 4 |
| 5 | | 3 | | | | | 6 | 1 | | 5 |
| 6 | 6 | 1 | | | 3 | | 2 | | 4 | 6 |
| 7 | | 6 | 2 | 1 | 9 | 3 | 5 | 8 | 8 | 7 |
| 8 | 8 | 1 | | 6 | | 7 | 4 | | 2 | 8 |
| 9 | | 7 | | 8 | | 8 | 4 | 6 | 1 | 9 |

Puzzle 5  Grid 4

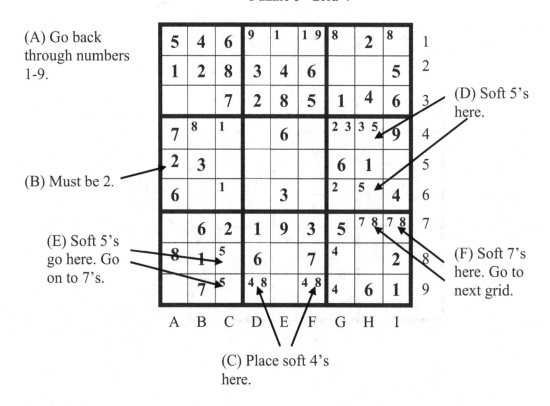

(A) Go back through numbers 1-9.

(B) Must be 2.

(E) Soft 5's go here. Go on to 7's.

(D) Soft 5's here.

(F) Soft 7's here. Go to next grid.

(C) Place soft 4's here.

Grid 4

| | A | B | C | D | E | F | G | H | I | |
|---|---|---|---|---|---|---|---|---|---|---|
| 1 | 5 | 4 | 6 | 9 / 1 | 1 9 | 8 | 2 | 8 | | 1 |
| 2 | 1 | 2 | 8 | 3 | 4 | 6 | | | 5 | 2 |
| 3 | | | 7 | 2 | 8 | 5 | 1 | 4 | 6 | 3 |
| 4 | 7 | 8 | 1 | | 6 | | 2 3 | 3 5 | 9 | 4 |
| 5 | 2 | 3 | | | | | 6 | 1 | | 5 |
| 6 | 6 | | 1 | | 3 | | 2 | 5 | 4 | 6 |
| 7 | | 6 | 2 | 1 | 9 | 3 | 5 | 7 8 | 7 8 | 7 |
| 8 | 8 | 1 | 5 | 6 | | 7 | 4 | | 2 | 8 |
| 9 | | 7 | 5 | 4 8 | | 4 8 | 4 | 6 | 1 | 9 |

We have placed a number of solid clues and soft clues. Use logic now to analyze the columns, boxes and rows for placement of additional clues.

Puzzle 5 Grid 5

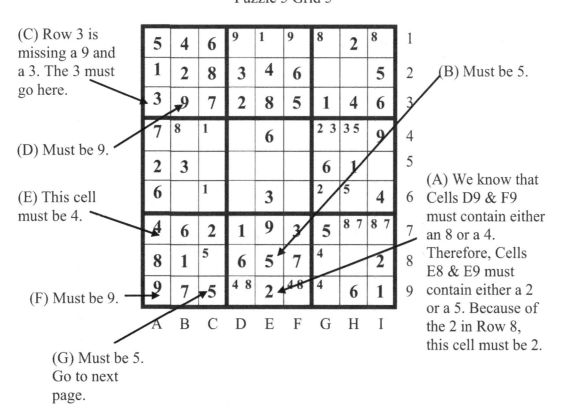

(C) Row 3 is missing a 9 and a 3. The 3 must go here.

(D) Must be 9.

(E) This cell must be 4.

(F) Must be 9.

(G) Must be 5. Go to next page.

(B) Must be 5.

(A) We know that Cells D9 & F9 must contain either an 8 or a 4. Therefore, Cells E8 & E9 must contain either a 2 or a 5. Because of the 2 in Row 8, this cell must be 2.

163

## Grid 5

| | A | B | C | D | E | F | G | H | I | |
|---|---|---|---|---|---|---|---|---|---|---|
| 1 | 5 | 4 | 6 | (9) | 1 | (9) | (8) | 2 | (8) | |
| 2 | 1 | 2 | 8 | 3 | 4 | 6 | | | 5 | |
| 3 | 3 | 9 | 7 | 2 | 8 | 5 | 1 | 4 | 6 | |
| 4 | 7 (8) | (1) | | | 6 | | (2 3) | (3 5) | 9 | |
| 5 | 2 | 3 | | | | | 6 | 1 | | |
| 6 | 6 | (1) | | | 3 | | (2) | (5) | 4 | |
| 7 | 4 | 6 | 2 | 1 | 9 | 3 | 5 | (8 7) | (8 7) | |
| 8 | 8 | 1 | (5) | 6 | 5 | 7 | (4) | | 2 | |
| 9 | 9 | 7 | 5 | (4 8) | 2 | (4 8) | (4) | 6 | 1 | |

## Puzzle 5  Grid 6

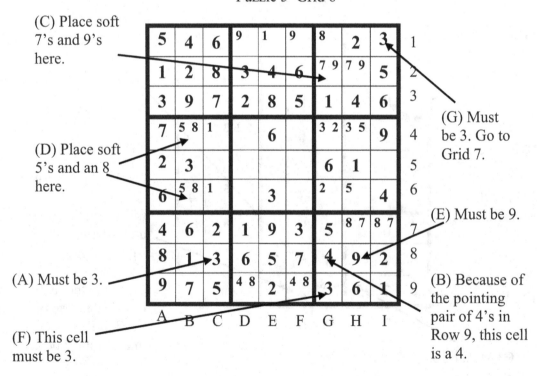

(C) Place soft 7's and 9's here.

(D) Place soft 5's and an 8 here.

(A) Must be 3.

(F) This cell must be 3.

(G) Must be 3. Go to Grid 7.

(E) Must be 9.

(B) Because of the pointing pair of 4's in Row 9, this cell is a 4.

164

## Grid 6

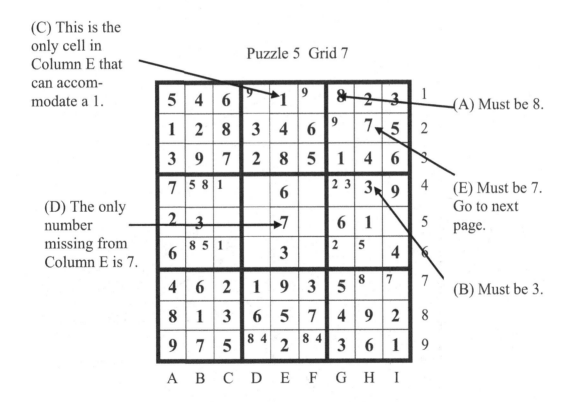

Grid 6 contents:

| | A | B | C | D | E | F | G | H | I | |
|---|---|---|---|---|---|---|---|---|---|---|
| 1 | 5 | 4 | 6 | ⁹ | ¹ | ⁹ | ⁸ | 2 | 3 | 1 |
| 2 | 1 | 2 | 8 | 3 | 4 | 6 | ⁷ ⁹ | ⁷ ⁹ | 5 | 2 |
| 3 | 3 | 9 | 7 | 2 | 8 | 5 | 1 | 4 | 6 | 3 |
| 4 | 7 | ⁵ ⁸ ¹ | | | 6 | | ³ ² | ³ ⁵ | 9 | 4 |
| 5 | 2 | 3 | | | | | 6 | 1 | | 5 |
| 6 | 6 | ⁵ ⁸ ¹ | | | 3 | | ² | ⁵ | 4 | 6 |
| 7 | 4 | 6 | 2 | 1 | 9 | 3 | 5 | ⁸ ⁷ | ⁸ ⁷ | 7 |
| 8 | 8 | 1 | 3 | 6 | 5 | 7 | 4 | 9 | 2 | 8 |
| 9 | 9 | 7 | 5 | ⁴ ⁸ | 2 | ⁴ ⁸ | 3 | 6 | 1 | 9 |

## Puzzle 5  Grid 7

(C) This is the only cell in Column E that can accommodate a 1.

(A) Must be 8.

(E) Must be 7. Go to next page.

(D) The only number missing from Column E is 7.

(B) Must be 3.

Grid 7 contents:

| | A | B | C | D | E | F | G | H | I | |
|---|---|---|---|---|---|---|---|---|---|---|
| 1 | 5 | 4 | 6 | ⁹ | 1 | ⁹ | 8 | 2 | 3 | 1 |
| 2 | 1 | 2 | 8 | 3 | 4 | 6 | ⁹ | 7 | 5 | 2 |
| 3 | 3 | 9 | 7 | 2 | 8 | 5 | 1 | 4 | 6 | 3 |
| 4 | 7 | ⁵ ⁸ ¹ | | | 6 | | ² ³ | 3 | 9 | 4 |
| 5 | 2 | 3 | | 7 | | | 6 | 1 | | 5 |
| 6 | 6 | ⁸ ⁵ ¹ | | | 3 | | ² | ⁵ | 4 | 6 |
| 7 | 4 | 6 | 2 | 1 | 9 | 3 | 5 | ⁸ | ⁷ | 7 |
| 8 | 8 | 1 | 3 | 6 | 5 | 7 | 4 | 9 | 2 | 8 |
| 9 | 9 | 7 | 5 | ⁸ ⁴ | 2 | ⁸ ⁴ | 3 | 6 | 1 | 9 |

## Grid 7

|   | A | B | C | D | E | F | G | H | I |   |
|---|---|---|---|---|---|---|---|---|---|---|
| 1 | 5 | 4 | 6 | ⁹ | 1 | ⁹ | 8 | 2 | 3 | 1 |
| 2 | 1 | 2 | 8 | 3 | 4 | 6 | ⁹ | 7 | 5 | 2 |
| 3 | 3 | 9 | 7 | 2 | 8 | 5 | 1 | 4 | 6 | 3 |
| 4 | 7 | ⁵⁸¹ |   |   | 6 |   | ²³ | 3 | 9 | 4 |
| 5 | 2 | 3 |   |   | 7 |   | 6 | 1 |   | 5 |
| 6 | 6 | ⁸⁵¹ |   |   | 3 |   | ² | ⁵ | 4 | 6 |
| 7 | 4 | 6 | 2 | 1 | 9 | 3 | 5 | ⁸ | ⁷ | 7 |
| 8 | 8 | 1 | 3 | 6 | 5 | 7 | 4 | 9 | 2 | 8 |
| 9 | 9 | 7 | 5 | ⁸⁴ | 2 | ⁸⁴ | 3 | 6 | 1 | 9 |

A B C D E F G H I

## Puzzle 5  Grid 8

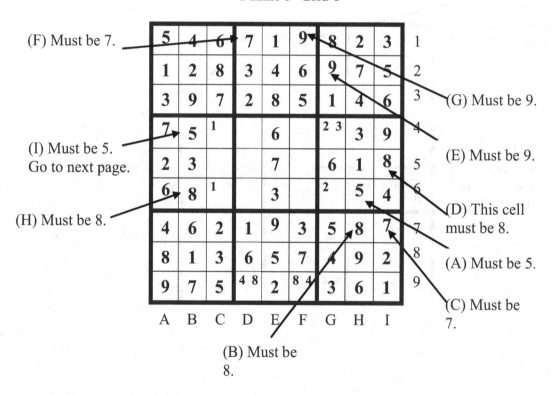

(F) Must be 7.

(G) Must be 9.

(I) Must be 5.
Go to next page.

(E) Must be 9.

(H) Must be 8.

(D) This cell must be 8.

(A) Must be 5.

(C) Must be 7.

(B) Must be 8.

166

## Grid 8

| | A | B | C | D | E | F | G | H | I |
|---|---|---|---|---|---|---|---|---|---|
| 1 | 5 | 4 | 6 | 7 | 1 | 9 | 8 | 2 | 3 |
| 2 | 1 | 2 | 8 | 3 | 4 | 6 | 9 | 7 | 5 |
| 3 | 3 | 9 | 7 | 2 | 8 | 5 | 1 | 4 | 6 |
| 4 | 7 | 5 | 1 | | 6 | | 2 3 | 3 | 9 |
| 5 | 2 | 3 | | | 7 | | 6 | 1 | 8 |
| 6 | 6 | 8 | 1 | | 3 | | 2 | 5 | 4 |
| 7 | 4 | 6 | 2 | 1 | 9 | 3 | 5 | 8 | 7 |
| 8 | 8 | 1 | 3 | 6 | 5 | 7 | 4 | 9 | 2 |
| 9 | 9 | 7 | 5 | 4 8 | 2 | 8 4 | 3 | 6 | 1 |

## Puzzle 5  Grid 9

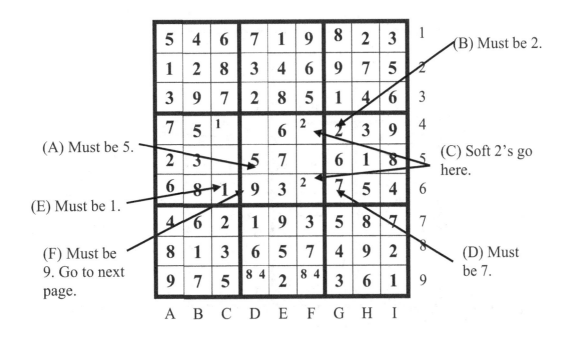

(B) Must be 2.

(A) Must be 5.

(C) Soft 2's go here.

(E) Must be 1.

(F) Must be 9. Go to next page.

(D) Must be 7.

167

Grid 9

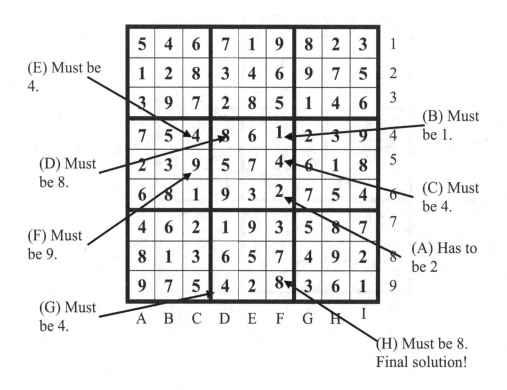

Puzzle 5 Grid 10
**Final Solution**

(E) Must be 4.

(D) Must be 8.

(F) Must be 9.

(G) Must be 4.

(B) Must be 1.

(C) Must be 4.

(A) Has to be 2

(H) Must be 8. Final solution!

## Worksheet for Puzzle 6

Cut along the dotted line to remove the worksheet.

| 4 |   |   | 8 |   | 3 |   |   |   |
|---|---|---|---|---|---|---|---|---|
|   |   |   |   | 9 | 4 |   | 7 | 3 |
|   |   | 3 |   |   |   |   | 5 | 6 |
|   |   |   |   | 8 | 7 |   |   | 2 |
|   |   | 5 |   |   |   | 7 |   |   |
| 6 |   |   | 5 | 1 |   |   |   |   |
| 2 | 1 |   |   |   |   | 9 |   |   |
| 9 | 5 |   | 7 | 6 |   |   |   |   |
|   |   |   | 9 |   | 8 |   |   | 5 |

## Puzzle 6

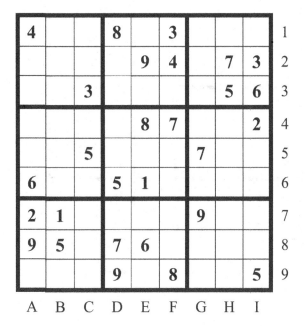

Puzzle 6  Grid 1

(C) Soft 1's go here.

(F) Soft 3's go here. Go to the next page.

(G) Soft 3's go here.

(E) Soft 2's go here.

(B) Soft 1's go here.

(A) This cell must be 1.

(D) Must be 2.

171

Grid 1

|   | A | B | C | D | E | F | G | H | I |   |
|---|---|---|---|---|---|---|---|---|---|---|
| 1 | 4 |   |   | 8 |   | 3 |   |   |   | 1 |
| 2 |   |   |   | 1 | 9 | 4 |   | 7 | 3 | 2 |
| 3 |   |   | 3 | 1 |   |   |   | 5 | 6 | 3 |
| 4 |   |   |   |   | 8 | 7 |   |   | 2 | 4 |
| 5 |   |   | 5 |   |   |   | 7 |   |   | 5 |
| 6 | 6 |   |   | 5 | 1 |   |   |   |   | 6 |
| 7 | 2 | 1 |   | 3 | 3 |   | 9 |   |   | 7 |
| 8 | 9 | 5 |   | 7 | 6 | 1 | 2 | 2 |   | 8 |
| 9 | 3 | 3 |   | 9 | 2 | 8 | 1 | 1 | 5 | 9 |

A  B  C  D  E  F  G  H  I

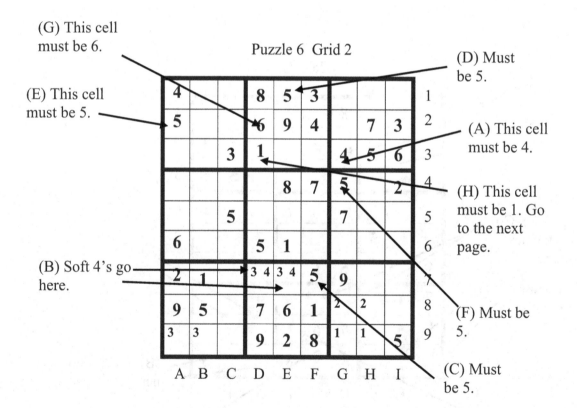

Puzzle 6  Grid 2

(G) This cell must be 6.

(E) This cell must be 5.

(D) Must be 5.

(A) This cell must be 4.

(H) This cell must be 1. Go to the next page.

(B) Soft 4's go here.

(F) Must be 5.

(C) Must be 5.

172

## Grid 2

| | A | B | C | D | E | F | G | H | I |
|---|---|---|---|---|---|---|---|---|---|
| 1 | 4 | | | 8 | 5 | 3 | | | |
| 2 | 5 | | | 6 | 9 | 4 | | 7 | 3 |
| 3 | | | 3 | 1 | | | 4 | 5 | 6 |
| 4 | | | | 8 | 7 | 5 | | | 2 |
| 5 | | | 5 | | | | 7 | | |
| 6 | 6 | | | 5 | 1 | | | | |
| 7 | 2 | 1 | | ³ ⁴ | ³ ⁴ | 5 | 9 | | |
| 8 | 9 | 5 | | 7 | 6 | 1 | ² | ² | |
| 9 | ³ | ³ | | 9 | 2 | 8 | ¹ | ¹ | 5 |

## Puzzle 6  Grid 3

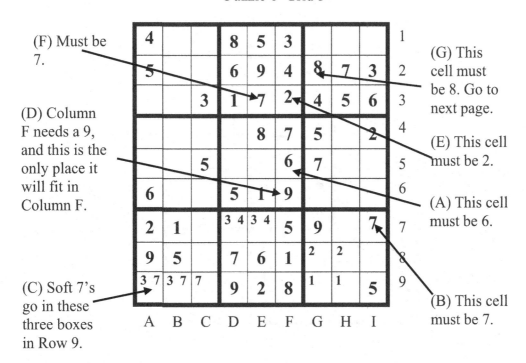

(F) Must be 7.

(D) Column F needs a 9, and this is the only place it will fit in Column F.

(C) Soft 7's go in these three boxes in Row 9.

(G) This cell must be 8. Go to next page.

(E) This cell must be 2.

(A) This cell must be 6.

(B) This cell must be 7.

173

Grid 3

Puzzle 6 Grid 4

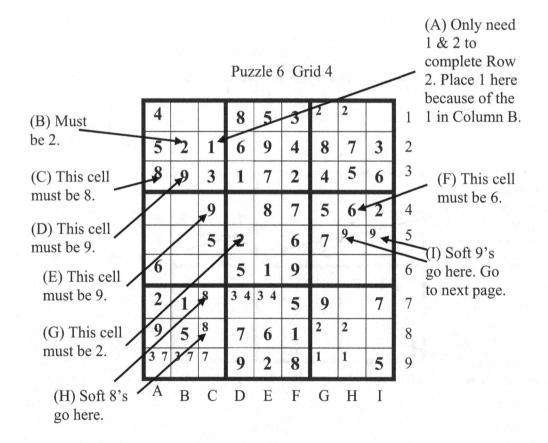

(A) Only need 1 & 2 to complete Row 2. Place 1 here because of the 1 in Column B.

(B) Must be 2.

(C) This cell must be 8.

(D) This cell must be 9.

(E) This cell must be 9.

(G) This cell must be 2.

(F) This cell must be 6.

(I) Soft 9's go here. Go to next page.

(H) Soft 8's go here.

174

Grid 4

| | A | B | C | D | E | F | G | H | I | |
|---|---|---|---|---|---|---|---|---|---|---|
| | 4 | | | 8 | 5 | 3 | 2 | 2 | | 1 |
| | 5 | 2 | 1 | 6 | 9 | 4 | 8 | 7 | 3 | 2 |
| | 8 | 9 | 3 | 1 | 7 | 2 | 4 | 5 | 6 | 3 |
| | | | 9 | | 8 | 7 | 5 | 6 | 2 | 4 |
| | | | 5 | 2 | | 6 | 7 | 9 | 9 | 5 |
| | 6 | | | 5 | 1 | 9 | | | | 6 |
| | 2 | 1 | 8 | 3 4 | 3 4 | 5 | 9 | | 7 | 7 |
| | 9 | 5 | 8 | 7 | 6 | 1 | 2 | 2 | | 8 |
| | 3 7 | 3 7 | 7 | 9 | 2 | 8 | 1 | 1 | 5 | 9 |

A  B  C  D  E  F  G  H  I

Puzzle 6  Grid 5

(A) Soft 2's here.

(B) This cell is the only cell in Row 4 that will accommodate a 1.

(C) Soft 1's here.

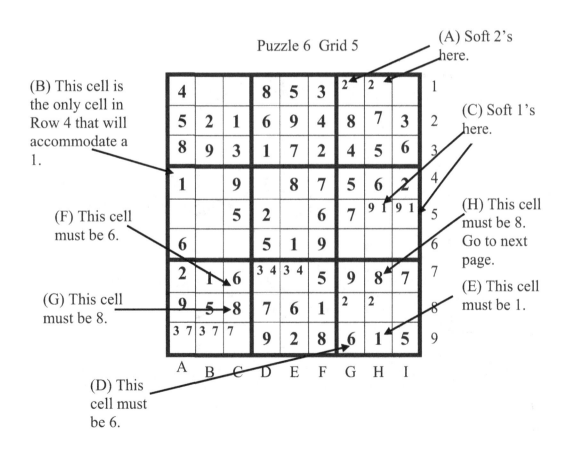

| | A | B | C | D | E | F | G | H | I | |
|---|---|---|---|---|---|---|---|---|---|---|
| | 4 | | | 8 | 5 | 3 | 2 | 2 | | 1 |
| | 5 | 2 | 1 | 6 | 9 | 4 | 8 | 7 | 3 | 2 |
| | 8 | 9 | 3 | 1 | 7 | 2 | 4 | 5 | 6 | 3 |
| | 1 | | 9 | | 8 | 7 | 5 | 6 | 2 | 4 |
| | | | 5 | 2 | | 6 | 7 | 9 1 | 9 1 | 5 |
| | 6 | | | 5 | 1 | 9 | | | | 6 |
| | 2 | 1 | 6 | 3 4 | 3 4 | 5 | 9 | 8 | 7 | 7 |
| | 9 | 5 | 8 | 7 | 6 | 1 | 2 | 2 | | 8 |
| | 3 7 | 3 7 | 7 | 9 | 2 | 8 | 6 | 1 | 5 | 9 |

A  B  C  D  E  F  G  H  I

(F) This cell must be 6.

(G) This cell must be 8.

(H) This cell must be 8. Go to next page.

(E) This cell must be 1.

(D) This cell must be 6.

Grid 5

| | A | B | C | D | E | F | G | H | I | |
|---|---|---|---|---|---|---|---|---|---|---|
| | 4 | | | 8 | 5 | 3 | ²_ | ²_ | | 1 |
| | 5 | 2 | 1 | 6 | 9 | 4 | 8 | 7 | 3 | 2 |
| | 8 | 9 | 3 | 1 | 7 | 2 | 4 | 5 | 6 | 3 |
| | 1 | | 9 | | 8 | 7 | 5 | 6 | 2 | 4 |
| | | | 5 | 2 | | 6 | 7 | ⁹¹_ | ⁹¹_ | 5 |
| | 6 | | | 5 | 1 | 9 | | | | 6 |
| | 2 | 1 | 6 | ³⁴_ | ³⁴_ | 5 | 9 | 8 | 7 | 7 |
| | 9 | 5 | 8 | 7 | 6 | 1 | ²_ | ²_ | | 8 |
| | ³⁷_ | ³⁷_ | ⁷_ | 9 | 2 | 8 | 6 | 1 | 5 | 9 |

Puzzle 6  Grid 6

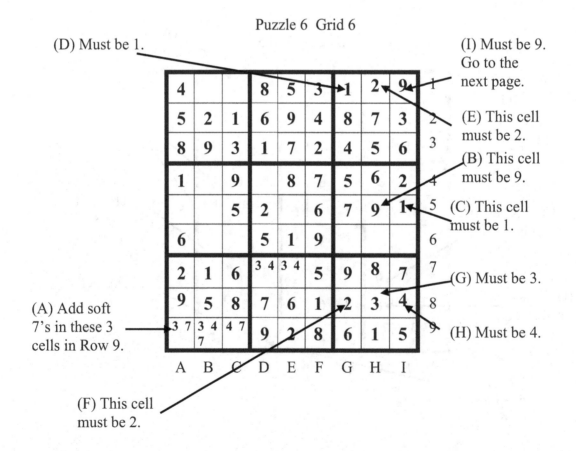

(D) Must be 1.

(I) Must be 9. Go to the next page.

(E) This cell must be 2.

(B) This cell must be 9.

(C) This cell must be 1.

(G) Must be 3.

(H) Must be 4.

(A) Add soft 7's in these 3 cells in Row 9.

(F) This cell must be 2.

176

## Grid 6

| | A | B | C | D | E | F | G | H | I | |
|---|---|---|---|---|---|---|---|---|---|---|
| 1 | 4 | | | 8 | 5 | 3 | 1 | 2 | 9 | 1 |
| 2 | 5 | 2 | 1 | 6 | 9 | 4 | 8 | 7 | 3 | 2 |
| 3 | 8 | 9 | 3 | 1 | 7 | 2 | 4 | 5 | 6 | 3 |
| 4 | 1 | | 9 | | 8 | 7 | 5 | 6 | 2 | 4 |
| 5 | | | 5 | 2 | | 6 | 7 | 9 | 1 | 5 |
| 6 | 6 | | | 5 | 1 | 9 | | | | 6 |
| 7 | 2 | 1 | 6 | 3 4 | 3 4 | 5 | 9 | 8 | 7 | 7 |
| 8 | 9 | 5 | 8 | 7 | 6 | 1 | 2 | 3 | 4 | 8 |
| 9 | 3 7 | 3 4 7 | 4 7 | 9 | 2 | 8 | 6 | 1 | 5 | 9 |

A  B  C  D  E  F  G  H  I

## Puzzle 6  Grid 7

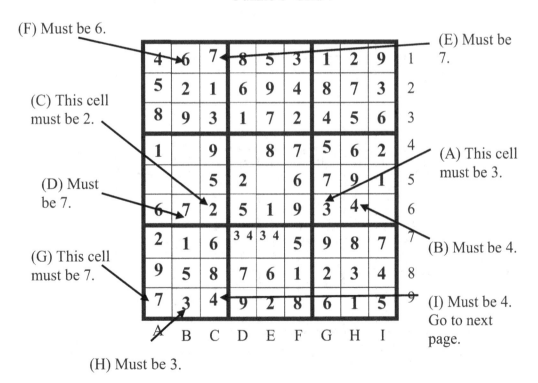

(F) Must be 6.

(E) Must be 7.

(C) This cell must be 2.

(A) This cell must be 3.

(D) Must be 7.

(B) Must be 4.

(G) This cell must be 7.

(I) Must be 4. Go to next page.

(H) Must be 3.

## Grid 7

|   | A | B | C | D | E | F | G | H | I |   |
|---|---|---|---|---|---|---|---|---|---|---|
| 1 | 4 | 6 | 7 | 8 | 5 | 3 | 1 | 2 | 9 | 1 |
| 2 | 5 | 2 | 1 | 6 | 9 | 4 | 8 | 7 | 3 | 2 |
| 3 | 8 | 9 | 3 | 1 | 7 | 2 | 4 | 5 | 6 | 3 |
| 4 | 1 |   | 9 |   | 8 | 7 | 5 | 6 | 2 | 4 |
| 5 |   |   | 5 | 2 |   | 6 | 7 | 9 | 1 | 5 |
| 6 | 6 | 7 | 2 | 5 | 1 | 9 | 3 | 4 |   | 6 |
| 7 | 2 | 1 | 6 | 3 4 | 3 4 | 5 | 9 | 8 | 7 | 7 |
| 8 | 9 | 5 | 8 | 7 | 6 | 1 | 2 | 3 | 4 | 8 |
| 9 | 7 | 3 | 4 | 9 | 2 | 8 | 6 | 1 | 5 | 9 |

A B C D E F G H I

Puzzle 6  Grid 8
**Final Solution**

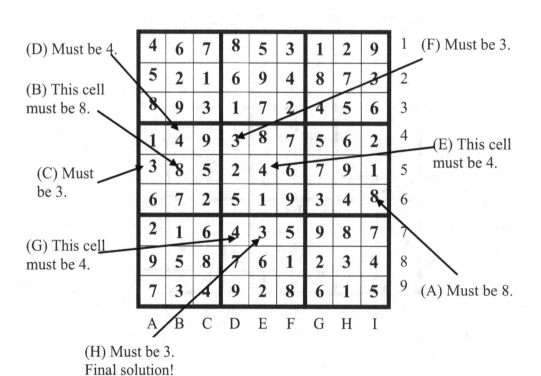

(D) Must be 4.

(B) This cell must be 8.

(C) Must be 3.

(G) This cell must be 4.

(F) Must be 3.

(E) This cell must be 4.

(A) Must be 8.

(H) Must be 3. Final solution!

| 3 | 2 | 7 |   |   |   |   |   |   |
|---|---|---|---|---|---|---|---|---|
|   | 1 |   |   | 3 |   | 5 | 7 |   |
|   |   | 5 | 7 | 1 |   | 2 |   |   |
| 2 |   | 4 |   |   | 8 |   |   | 7 |
|   |   |   |   |   |   |   |   |   |
| 1 |   |   | 6 |   |   | 4 |   | 5 |
|   |   | 1 |   | 2 | 7 | 6 |   |   |
|   | 5 | 9 |   | 6 |   |   |   |   |
|   |   |   |   |   |   | 1 | 3 | 4 |

## *Puzzle 7*

|   | A | B | C | D | E | F | G | H | I |   |
|---|---|---|---|---|---|---|---|---|---|---|
| 1 | 3 | 2 | 7 |   |   |   |   |   |   | 1 |
| 2 |   | 1 |   |   | 3 |   | 5 | 7 |   | 2 |
| 3 |   |   | 5 | 7 | 1 |   | 2 |   |   | 3 |
| 4 | 2 |   | 4 |   |   | 8 |   |   | 7 | 4 |
| 5 |   |   |   |   |   |   |   |   |   | 5 |
| 6 | 1 |   |   | 6 |   |   | 4 |   | 5 | 6 |
| 7 |   |   | 1 |   | 2 | 7 | 6 |   |   | 7 |
| 8 |   | 5 | 9 |   | 6 |   |   |   |   | 8 |
| 9 |   |   |   |   |   |   | 1 | 3 | 4 | 9 |

Using "speed sudoku" techniques, place hard and soft clues working systematically 1-9.

### Puzzle 7  Grid 1

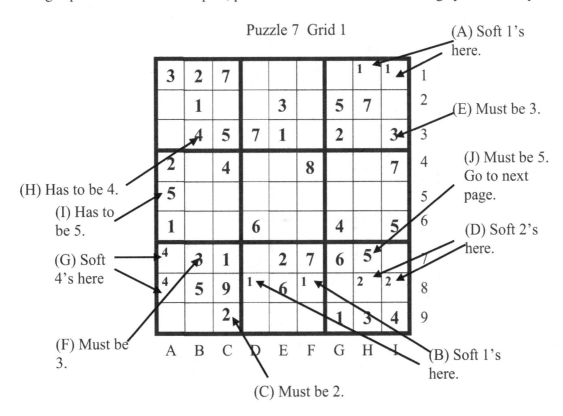

(A) Soft 1's here.

(E) Must be 3.

(J) Must be 5. Go to next page.

(H) Has to be 4.

(I) Has to be 5.

(G) Soft 4's here

(D) Soft 2's here.

(F) Must be 3.

(B) Soft 1's here.

(C) Must be 2.

Grid 1

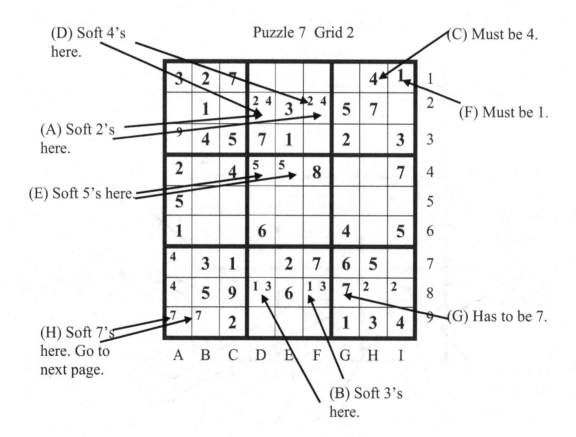

Puzzle 7  Grid 2

(D) Soft 4's here.

(C) Must be 4.

(A) Soft 2's here.

(F) Must be 1.

(E) Soft 5's here.

(H) Soft 7's here. Go to next page.

(G) Has to be 7.

(B) Soft 3's here.

182

|   | A | B | C | D | E | F | G | H | I |   |
|---|---|---|---|---|---|---|---|---|---|---|
| 1 | 3 | 2 | 7 |   |   |   |   | 4 | 1 | 1 |
| 2 |   | 1 |   | 2 4 | 3 | 2 4 | 5 | 7 |   | 2 |
| 3 | 9 | 4 | 5 | 7 | 1 |   | 2 |   | 3 | 3 |
| 4 | 2 |   | 4 | 5 | 5 | 8 |   |   | 7 | 4 |
| 5 | 5 |   |   |   |   |   |   |   |   | 5 |
| 6 | 1 |   |   | 6 |   |   | 4 |   | 5 | 6 |
| 7 | 4 | 3 | 1 |   | 2 | 7 | 6 | 5 |   | 7 |
| 8 | 4 | 5 | 9 | 1 3 | 6 | 1 3 | 7 | 2 | 2 | 8 |
| 9 | 7 | 7 | 2 |   |   |   | 1 | 3 | 4 | 9 |

Puzzle 7  Grid 3

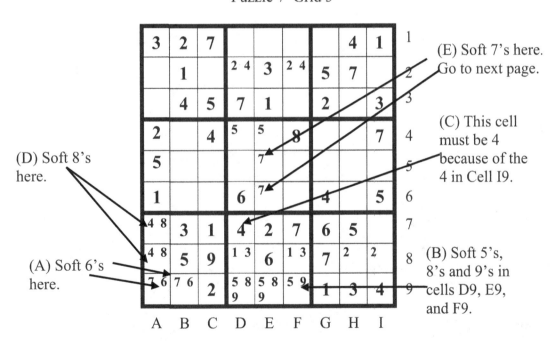

(E) Soft 7's here. Go to next page.

(C) This cell must be 4 because of the 4 in Cell I9.

(D) Soft 8's here.

(A) Soft 6's here.

(B) Soft 5's, 8's and 9's in cells D9, E9, and F9.

Grid 3

Puzzle 7  Grid 4

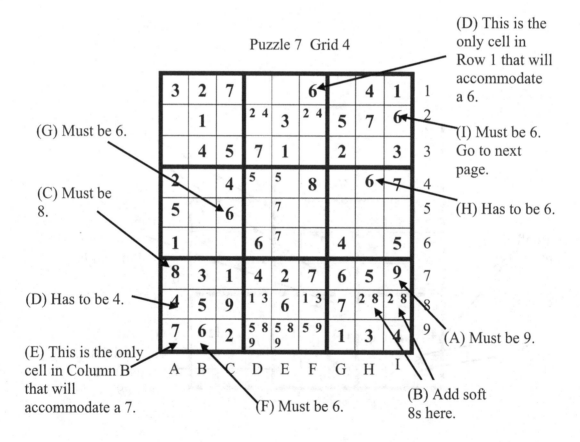

(D) This is the only cell in Row 1 that will accommodate a 6.

(I) Must be 6. Go to next page.

(H) Has to be 6.

(G) Must be 6.

(C) Must be 8.

(D) Has to be 4.

(E) This is the only cell in Column B that will accommodate a 7.

(F) Must be 6.

(A) Must be 9.

(B) Add soft 8s here.

Grid 4

(C) Must be 8.

Puzzle 7  Grid 5

(B) Must be 9.

(F) Must be 1.

(A) Must be 6.

(G) Has to be 5.
Go to next page.

(E) Must be 1.

(D) Must be 3.

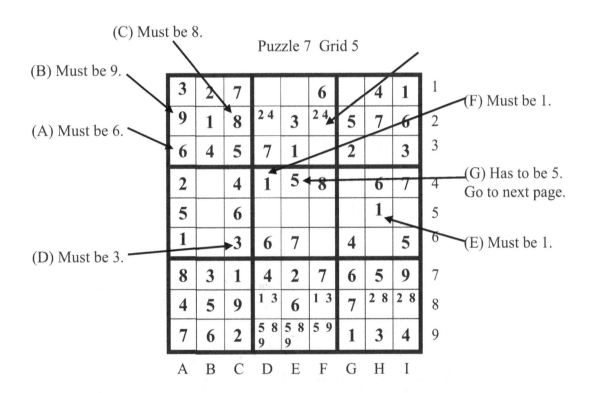

Grid 5

| | A | B | C | D | E | F | G | H | I | |
|---|---|---|---|---|---|---|---|---|---|---|
| | 3 | 2 | 7 | | | 6 | | 4 | 1 | 1 |
| | 9 | 1 | 8 | 2 4 | 3 | 2 4 | 5 | 7 | 6 | 2 |
| | 6 | 4 | 5 | 7 | 1 | | 2 | | 3 | 3 |
| | 2 | | 4 | 1 | 5 | 8 | | 6 | 7 | 4 |
| | 5 | | 6 | | | | | 1 | | 5 |
| | 1 | | 3 | 6 | 7 | | 4 | | 5 | 6 |
| | 8 | 3 | 1 | 4 | 2 | 7 | 6 | 5 | 9 | 7 |
| | 4 | 5 | 9 | 3 1 | 6 | 1 3 | 7 | 2 8 | 8 2 | 8 |
| | 7 | 6 | 2 | 5 8 9 | 5 8 9 | 5 9 | 1 | 3 | 4 | 9 |

A  B  C  D  E  F  G  H  I

Puzzle 7  Grid 6

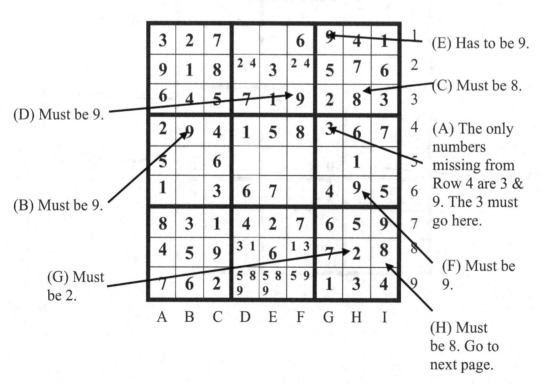

(E) Has to be 9.

(C) Must be 8.

(D) Must be 9.

(A) The only numbers missing from Row 4 are 3 & 9. The 3 must go here.

(B) Must be 9.

(F) Must be 9.

(G) Must be 2.

(H) Must be 8. Go to next page.

186

## Grid 6

| | | | | | | | | | |
|---|---|---|---|---|---|---|---|---|---|
| 3 | 2 | 7 | | | 6 | 9 | 4 | 1 | 1 |
| 9 | 1 | 8 | 2 4 | 3 | 2 4 | 5 | 7 | 6 | 2 |
| 6 | 4 | 5 | 7 | 1 | 9 | 2 | 8 | 3 | 3 |
| 2 | 9 | 4 | 1 | 5 | 8 | 3 | 6 | 7 | 4 |
| 5 | | 6 | | | | | 1 | | 5 |
| 1 | | 3 | 6 | 7 | | 4 | 9 | 5 | 6 |
| 8 | 3 | 1 | 4 | 2 | 7 | 6 | 5 | 9 | 7 |
| 4 | 5 | 9 | 3 1 | 6 | 3 1 | 7 | 2 | 8 | 8 |
| 7 | 6 | 2 | 5 8 9 | 5 8 9 | 5 9 | 1 | 3 | 4 | 9 |

A   B   C   D   E   F   G   H   I

## Puzzle 7  Grid 7

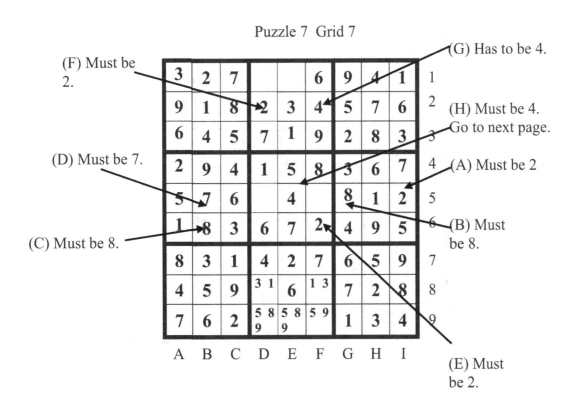

(F) Must be 2.

(G) Has to be 4.

(H) Must be 4. Go to next page.

(A) Must be 2

(D) Must be 7.

(B) Must be 8.

(C) Must be 8.

(E) Must be 2.

187

Grid 7

| A | B | C | D | E | F | G | H | I | |
|---|---|---|---|---|---|---|---|---|---|
| 3 | 2 | 7 |   |   | 6 | 9 | 4 | 1 | 1 |
| 9 | 1 | 8 | 2 | 3 | 4 | 5 | 7 | 6 | 2 |
| 6 | 4 | 5 | 7 | 1 | 9 | 2 | 8 | 3 | 3 |
| 2 | 9 | 4 | 1 | 5 | 8 | 3 | 6 | 7 | 4 |
| 5 | 7 | 6 |   | 4 |   | 8 | 1 | 2 | 5 |
| 1 | 8 | 3 | 6 | 7 | 2 | 4 | 9 | 5 | 6 |
| 8 | 3 | 1 | 4 | 2 | 7 | 6 | 5 | 9 | 7 |
| 4 | 5 | 9 | 3 1 | 6 | 3 1 | 7 | 2 | 8 | 8 |
| 7 | 6 | 2 | 5 8 9 | 5 8 9 | 5 9 | 1 | 3 | 4 | 9 |

Puzzle 7  Grid 8
**Final Solution**

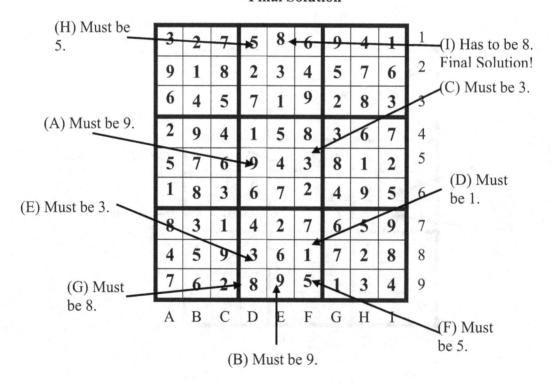

(H) Must be 5.

(I) Has to be 8. Final Solution!

(C) Must be 3.

(A) Must be 9.

(D) Must be 1.

(E) Must be 3.

(G) Must be 8.

(F) Must be 5.

(B) Must be 9.

188

# Other Techniques for Solving

The following two techniques are well documented in other Sudoku publications but are extremely esoteric and rarely used. The first is the *XYZ Wing*. This technique is difficult to spot and use in solving a puzzle. I have solved thousands of Sudoku puzzles and have only used it once or twice. *Wings and Swordfish* are even more esoteric and less useful in solving a puzzle. Likewise, I have rarely used these techniques in solving an actual puzzle. Only cursory instruction will be given on these solving techniques because of their cumbersome nature and the rarity of their use.

## XYZ Wing Technique

In puzzles that have been reduced to the point that simple solving techniques won't work, employ more complex methods. The XYZ Wing technique always involves three numbers in two columns and two rows. In the sample below, the 3 and 4 in Cell A1 serve as the X-Y, or 'stem', of the wing (see shaded portions of the Sudoku square). The 8 in Cells A5 and H1 serve as the Z part, or 'branch', of the wing. Thus, any 8's found in Column H or Row 5 can be eliminated.

| A | B | C | D | E | F | G | H | I | |
|---|---|---|---|---|---|---|---|---|---|
| 3 4 | 1 | 7 |  | 5 | 6 | 2 | 3 8 | 4 | 1 |
| 8 2 | 5 | 3 4 | 1 9 | 3 | 2 | 6 | 7 | 3 8 | 2 |
| 9 3 1 8 2 | 8 2 | 6 | 4 |  | 7 | 9 3 5 | 5 3 | 9 5 | 3 |
| 7 | 3 4 | 2 | 6 | 148 | 5 | 9 | 1 4 | 148 | 4 |
| 4 8 | 9 | 4 8 | 2 7 | 2 7 | 3 | 5 | 148 | 6 | 5 |
| 5 | 6 | 1 3 4 8 | 8 | 4 | 9 | 7 | 2 | 3 | 6 |
| 1 | 3 4 | 9 | 5 | 2 7 | 8 |  | 6 | 7 | 7 |
| 8 2 | 7 | 5 | 3 | 6 | 4 | 8 1 2 | 8 1 2 |  | 8 |
| 6 | 8 2 | 3 4 | 2 7 | 9 | 1 | 4 | 5 | 8 | 9 |

A  B  C  D  E  F  G  H  I

189

## Wings and Swordfish

Wings and Swordfish are generic terms describing candidate or soft clue arrangements in a grid. They can be usful in solving difficult puzzles and, again, are not 100% fail safe.

|  | A | B | C | D | E | F | G | H | I |  |
|---|---|---|---|---|---|---|---|---|---|---|
| 1 | 7 6 | 5 | 2 | 9 7 6 | 8 7 6 | 3 | 1 | 4 | 7 6 | 1 |
| 2 | 8 3 | 1 | 3 8 | 249 | 249 | 249 5 6 | 6 9 | 5 7 | 3 8 | 2 |
| 3 |  | 4 | 7 6 | 1 | 5 |  | 3 | 2 |  | 3 |
| 4 | 5 6 7 | 5 6 7 | 8 | 2 4 | 2 4 5 6 | 1 | 9 2 4 | 5 6 7 | 123 | 4 |
| 5 | 5 2 4 | 3 | 1 | 2 4 9 | 2 4 8 |  |  |  |  | 5 |
| 6 |  | 2 | 9 | 7 | 3 4 |  | 5 | 8 | 1 | 6 |
| 7 | 123 | 6 7 | 6 7 | 5 | 2 4 8 |  | 2 4 6 | 1 | 9 | 7 |
| 8 |  | 8 | 5 |  | 1 |  |  |  |  | 8 |
| 9 | 1 | 9 | 4 | 6 7 | 6 9 |  | 8 | 3 |  | 9 |

In the example above, the 6/7 combinations in the shaded boxes form a wing, which can be used to eliminate the 6's and 7's located between the pairs.

Swordfish operate much the same way. These techniques can be useful, but are not infallible.

# Creating Your Own Sudoku Puzzles

While hundreds of Sudoku books have been written, to my knowledge this book is the most definitive comprehensive publication on solving the puzzles. This section of the book is devoted to teaching the readers how to construct Sudoku puzzles on their own. The tools required are:

1) Several blank grids
2) A number two pencil with a good eraser
3) Patience
4) Excellent puzzle solving skills

Begin by constructing the solution grid. Follow the steps on the following pages.

**A)** Select and place pairs of numbers in the top three boxes. The pairs selected in the example are 9 and 1, 7 and 4, and 6 and 5. Place them in alternating rows so that the first grid looks like this:

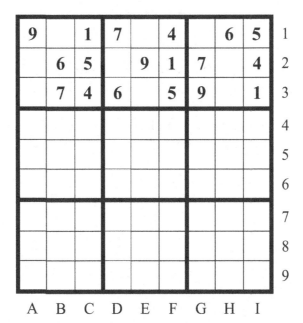

**B)** It doesn't matter in which cells these pairs are placed, as long as they share the same box and row.

**C)** The three numbers missing from these boxes are 2, 3 and 8. Place these three numbers so that each one is paired with one of the other pairs from Step A. In the diagram below, they are the numbers in parentheses.

|   | A | B | C | D | E | F | G | H | I |   |
|---|---|---|---|---|---|---|---|---|---|---|
| 1 | 9 | (2) | 1 | 7 | (3) | 4 | (8) | 6 | 5 | 1 |
| 2 | (3) | 6 | 5 | (8) | 9 | 1 | 7 | (2) | 4 | 2 |
| 3 | (8) | 7 | 4 | 6 | (2) | 5 | 9 | (3) | 1 | 3 |
| 4 |   |   |   |   |   |   |   |   |   | 4 |
| 5 |   |   |   |   |   |   |   |   |   | 5 |
| 6 |   |   |   |   |   |   |   |   |   | 6 |
| 7 |   |   |   |   |   |   |   |   |   | 7 |
| 8 |   |   |   |   |   |   |   |   |   | 8 |
| 9 |   |   |   |   |   |   |   |   |   | 9 |

A    B    C    D    E    F    G    H    I

**D)** Each number should be placed with a different number pair in each box. Note the highlighted cells above to see how this was done with the number 2.

**E)** The top three boxes are complete. Remember, however, that all the numbers just placed are subject to change until the entire solution grid is completed.

**F)** Now, repeat the process used in Steps A through E in the middle three boxes. (See grid on the next page.) This time, use different number pairs: 2 and 6, 5 and 8, and 9 and 3.

| | A | B | C | D | E | F | G | H | I | |
|---|---|---|---|---|---|---|---|---|---|---|
| | 9 | 2 | 1 | 7 | 3 | 4 | 8 | 6 | 5 | 1 |
| | 3 | 6 | 5 | 8 | 9 | 1 | 7 | 2 | 4 | 2 |
| | 8 | 7 | 4 | 6 | 2 | 5 | 9 | 3 | 1 | 3 |
| | 2 | | 6 | 5 | | 8 | | 9 | 3 | 4 |
| | | 9 | 3 | 2 | 6 | | | 5 | 8 | 5 |
| | 5 | | 8 | 9 | | 3 | 6 | | 2 | 6 |
| | | | | | | | | | | 7 |
| | | | | | | | | | | 8 |
| | | | | | | | | | | 9 |

A    B    C    D    E    F    G    H    I

**G)** The pairs have been placed in the middle boxes so that they comply with standard Sudoku rules (i.e. no duplications of digits 1 through 9 in any row, column or box). The numbers missing from the middle boxes are 1, 4 and 7. Now place these numbers so that each is placed with one of the previously placed pairs. The new numbers are in the parentheses in the next diagram. Manipulate any previously placed numbers so the Sudoku rules are met and that no mistakes are made.

**H)** Note, the position of 7 and 4 in the upper left box have been switched in order to comply with Sudoku rules. The cells are highlighted above.

**I)** Now begin working on the lower three boxes starting with the lower middle box. As the instructions become more detailed at this point, I outline each step with arrows on the next diagrams.

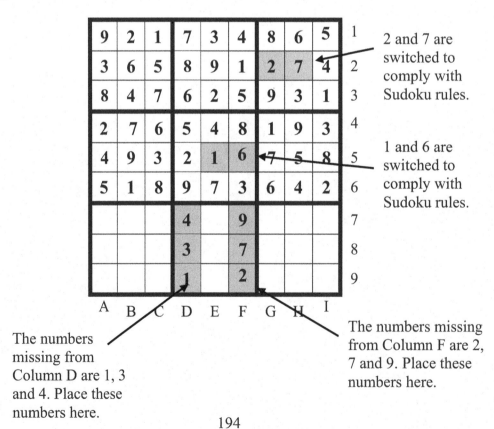

2 and 7 are switched to comply with Sudoku rules.

1 and 6 are switched to comply with Sudoku rules.

The numbers missing from Column D are 1, 3 and 4. Place these numbers here.

The numbers missing from Column F are 2, 7 and 9. Place these numbers here.

The numbers missing from Column E and the lower middle box are 5, 6 & 8.

The numbers missing from Column I are 6, 7 & 9. Place these numbers here.

| A | B | C | D | E | F | G | H | I | |
|---|---|---|---|---|---|---|---|---|---|
| 9 | 2 | 1 | 7 | 3 | 4 | 8 | 6 | 5 | 1 |
| 3 | 6 | 5 | 8 | 9 | 1 | 2 | 7 | 4 | 2 |
| 8 | 4 | 7 | 6 | 2 | 5 | 9 | 3 | 1 | 3 |
| 2 | 7 | 6 | 5 | 4 | 8 | 1 | 9 | 3 | 4 |
| 4 | 9 | 3 | 2 | 1 | 6 | 7 | 5 | 8 | 5 |
| 5 | 1 | 8 | 9 | 7 | 3 | 6 | 4 | 2 | 6 |
|   |   |   | 4 | 8 | 9 |   |   | 6 | 7 |
|   |   |   | 3 | 5 | 7 |   |   | 9 | 8 |
|   |   |   | 1 | 6 | 2 |   |   | 7 | 9 |

(A) The numbers mssing from Column G are 3, 4 & 5. Place these numbers here.

(B) Place the missing numbers, 8, 2 & 1, in this column. Go to next page.

| A | B | C | D | E | F | G | H | I | |
|---|---|---|---|---|---|---|---|---|---|
| 9 | 2 | 1 | 7 | 3 | 4 | 8 | 6 | 5 | 1 |
| 3 | 6 | 5 | 8 | 9 | 1 | 2 | 7 | 4 | 2 |
| 8 | 4 | 7 | 6 | 2 | 5 | 9 | 3 | 1 | 3 |
| 2 | 7 | 6 | 5 | 4 | 8 | 1 | 9 | 3 | 4 |
| 4 | 9 | 3 | 2 | 1 | 6 | 7 | 5 | 8 | 5 |
| 5 | 1 | 8 | 9 | 7 | 3 | 6 | 4 | 2 | 6 |
|   |   |   | 4 | 8 | 9 | 5 | 8 | 6 | 7 |
|   |   |   | 3 | 5 | 7 | 3 | 2 | 9 | 8 |
|   |   |   | 1 | 6 | 2 | 4 | 1 | 7 | 9 |

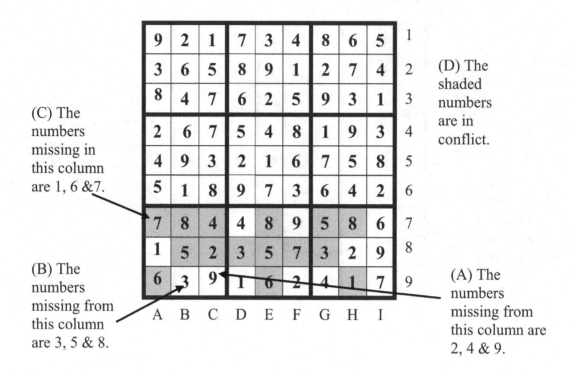

(C) The numbers missing in this column are 1, 6 & 7.

(B) The numbers missing from this column are 3, 5 & 8.

(D) The shaded numbers are in conflict.

(A) The numbers missing from this column are 2, 4 & 9.

| | | | | | | | | | |
|---|---|---|---|---|---|---|---|---|---|
| 9 | 2 | 1 | 7 | 3 | 4 | 8 | 6 | 5 | 1 |
| 3 | 6 | 5 | 8 | 9 | 1 | 2 | 7 | 4 | 2 |
| 8 | 4 | 7 | 6 | 2 | 5 | 9 | 3 | 1 | 3 |
| 2 | 7 | 6 | 5 | 4 | 8 | 1 | 9 | 3 | 4 |
| 4 | 9 | 3 | 2 | 1 | 6 | 7 | 5 | 8 | 5 |
| 5 | 1 | 8 | 9 | 7 | 3 | 6 | 4 | 2 | 6 |
| | | | 4 | | 9 | | | 6 | 7 |
| 1 | | | | | | | 2 | | 8 |
| | 3 | 9 | 1 | | 2 | 4 | | | 9 |

A  B  C  D  E  F  G  H  I

We erase the numbers in conflict and also some random numbers from the bottom 3 boxes and solve using Master Sudoku techniques. Go to next page.

196

Now solve the remaining cells using Master Sudoku techniques. Be patient! It might require several tries before you find the solution to the bottom 3 boxes.

|   | A | B | C | D | E | F | G | H | I |   |
|---|---|---|---|---|---|---|---|---|---|---|
| 1 | 9 | 2 | 1 | 7 | 3 | 4 | 8 | 6 | 5 | 1 |
| 2 | 3 | 6 | 5 | 8 | 9 | 1 | 2 | 7 | 4 | 2 |
| 3 | 8 | 4 | 7 | 6 | 2 | 5 | 9 | 3 | 1 | 3 |
| 4 | 2 | 7 | 6 | 5 | 4 | 8 | 1 | 9 | 3 | 4 |
| 5 | 4 | 9 | 3 | 2 | 1 | 6 | 7 | 5 | 8 | 5 |
| 6 | 5 | 1 | 8 | 9 | 7 | 3 | 6 | 4 | 2 | 6 |
| 7 |   |   |   | 4 |   | 9 |   |   | 6 | 7 |
| 8 | 1 |   |   |   |   |   |   | 2 |   | 8 |
| 9 |   | 3 | 9 | 1 |   | 2 | 4 |   |   | 9 |

(Below: A B C D E F G H I)

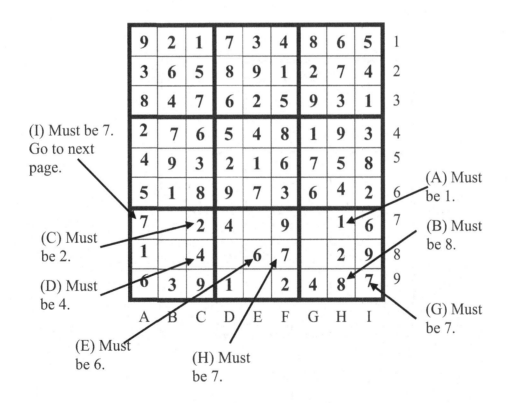

(I) Must be 7. Go to next page.

(C) Must be 2.

(D) Must be 4.

(E) Must be 6.

(H) Must be 7.

(A) Must be 1.

(B) Must be 8.

(G) Must be 7.

197

|   | A | B | C | D | E | F | G | H | I |   |
|---|---|---|---|---|---|---|---|---|---|---|
| 1 | 9 | 2 | 1 | 7 | 3 | 4 | 8 | 6 | 5 | 1 |
| 2 | 3 | 6 | 5 | 8 | 9 | 1 | 2 | 7 | 4 | 2 |
| 3 | 8 | 4 | 7 | 6 | 2 | 5 | 9 | 3 | 1 | 3 |
| 4 | 2 | 7 | 6 | 5 | 4 | 8 | 1 | 9 | 3 | 4 |
| 5 | 4 | 9 | 3 | 2 | 1 | 6 | 7 | 5 | 8 | 5 |
| 6 | 5 | 1 | 8 | 9 | 7 | 3 | 6 | 4 | 2 | 6 |
| 7 | 7 |   | 2 | 4 |   | 9 |   | 1 | 6 | 7 |
| 8 | 1 |   | 4 |   | 6 | 7 |   | 2 | 9 | 8 |
| 9 | 6 | 3 | 9 | 1 |   | 2 | 4 | 8 | 7 | 9 |

A  B  C  D  E  F  G  H  I

Now to create the beginning grid of a new puzzle, simply remove numbers or clues from the above grid. On the following pages, there are two different puzzle options that can be created with the solution below.

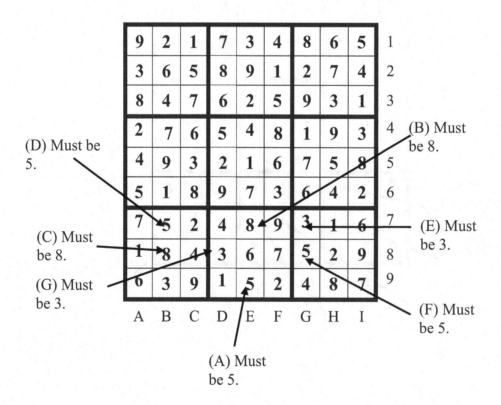

(D) Must be 5.

(B) Must be 8.

(C) Must be 8.

(E) Must be 3.

(G) Must be 3.

(F) Must be 5.

(A) Must be 5.

198

## New Puzzle 1

Eliminate the numbers from the solution grid on the previous page to create the puzzle below.

Remember, the degree of difficulty is inversely proportional to the number of clues used in the beginning grid. In other words, the larger the number of given clues used in the beginning grid – the easier the puzzle. The two example puzzles have 25 clues. Not as difficult as some puzzles you have solved in this book, but certainly challenging puzzles.

| A | B | C | D | E | F | G | H | I | |
|---|---|---|---|---|---|---|---|---|---|
|   | 2 |   | 7 |   | 4 |   |   |   | 1 |
|   | 6 |   | 8 | 9 |   | 2 |   |   | 2 |
| 8 |   |   |   | 2 |   |   |   |   | 3 |
|   |   |   | 5 | 4 |   | 1 |   | 3 | 4 |
|   | 9 |   |   | 1 |   |   | 5 |   | 5 |
|   |   | 8 |   |   |   |   | 4 |   | 6 |
|   |   |   |   |   |   |   | 1 | 6 | 7 |
|   | 8 |   | 3 | 6 | 7 |   |   |   | 8 |
|   |   |   |   |   |   |   | 8 |   | 9 |

A   B   C   D   E   F   G   H   I

# New Puzzle 2

Remove different numbers from the solutions grid to form a completed different puzzle.

This puzzle has also has 25 clues to help solve it.

| A | B | C | D | E | F | G | H | I |   |
|---|---|---|---|---|---|---|---|---|---|
| 9 |   |   | 3 |   |   |   |   |   | 1 |
|   |   |   | 8 | 9 |   |   |   | 4 | 2 |
|   |   |   |   |   |   |   |   |   | 3 |
|   | 7 | 6 | 5 |   | 8 |   |   |   | 4 |
|   |   |   |   |   |   | 7 | 5 | 8 | 5 |
|   |   |   |   |   | 3 |   |   |   | 6 |
|   | 5 |   | 4 |   |   | 3 | 1 |   | 7 |
|   | 8 |   |   | 6 |   |   |   |   | 8 |
| 6 |   |   | 1 | 5 |   |   | 8 | 7 | 9 |

## A Different Approach

Here is a faster way to reach a solution to the three bottom boxes. The grid below can have many different solutions for the bottom three boxes. Notice below, three possible solution grids for those boxes. All three are viable solution grids. Once the top six boxes are completed correctly, the bottom three boxes can have many possible number combinations.

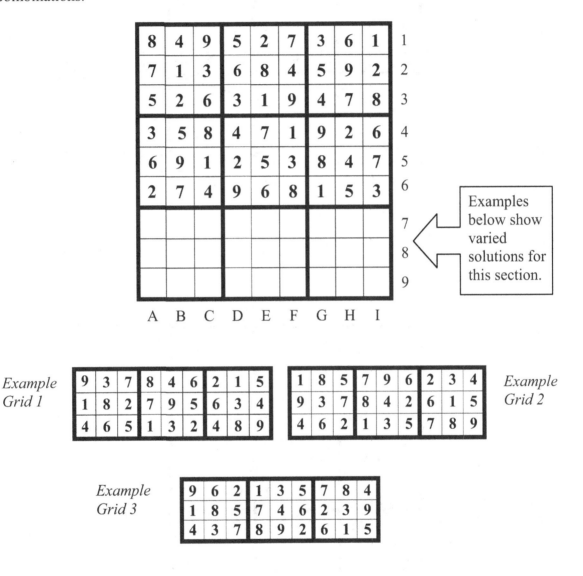

Follow the steps starting on the next page to learn the most expedient way to find one of the possible completions for the solution grid.

## Grid 1

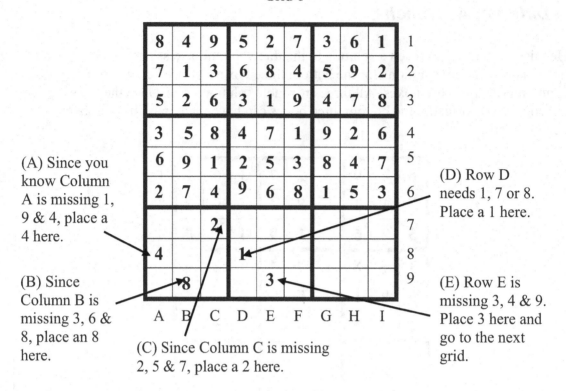

(A) Since you know Column A is missing 1, 9 & 4, place a 4 here.

(B) Since Column B is missing 3, 6 & 8, place an 8 here.

(C) Since Column C is missing 2, 5 & 7, place a 2 here.

(D) Row D needs 1, 7 or 8. Place a 1 here.

(E) Row E is missing 3, 4 & 9. Place 3 here and go to the next grid.

## Grid 2

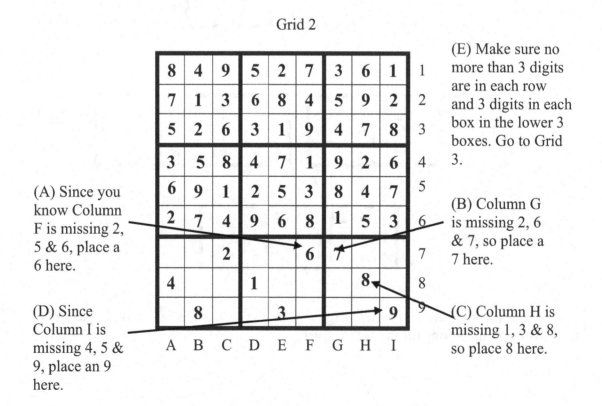

(A) Since you know Column F is missing 2, 5 & 6, place a 6 here.

(D) Since Column I is missing 4, 5 & 9, place an 9 here.

(B) Column G is missing 2, 6 & 7, so place a 7 here.

(C) Column H is missing 1, 3 & 8, so place 8 here.

(E) Make sure no more than 3 digits are in each row and 3 digits in each box in the lower 3 boxes. Go to Grid 3.

The order in which the numbers are placed in the bottom three boxes doesn't matter, nor does it matter which numbers are chosen. Just make sure to place them in compliance with Sudoku rules. Try to incorporate as many different digits as possible and spread them out.

Now solve the remaining cells using Speed Sudoku techniques. Go to Step A.

Grid 3

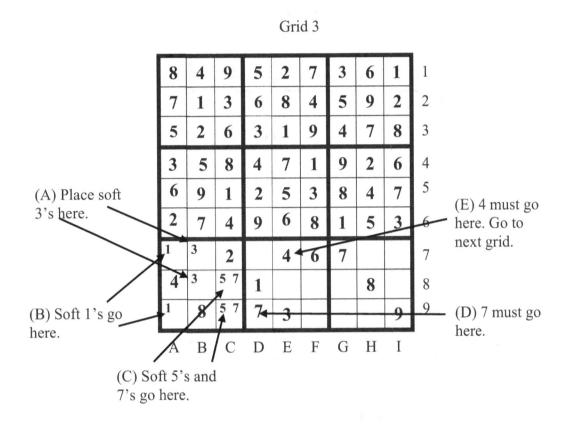

(A) Place soft 3's here.

(B) Soft 1's go here.

(C) Soft 5's and 7's go here.

(E) 4 must go here. Go to next grid.

(D) 7 must go here.

Grid 4

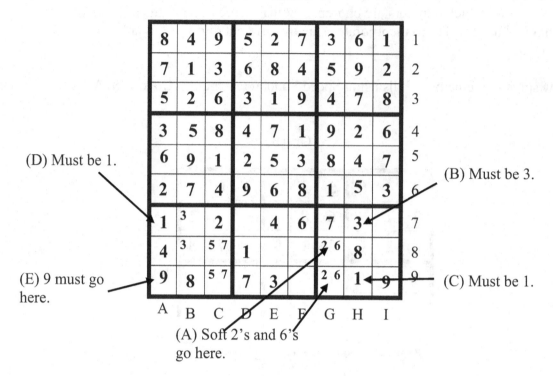

(D) Must be 1.

(B) Must be 3.

(E) 9 must go here.

(C) Must be 1.

(A) Soft 2's and 6's go here.

Grid 5

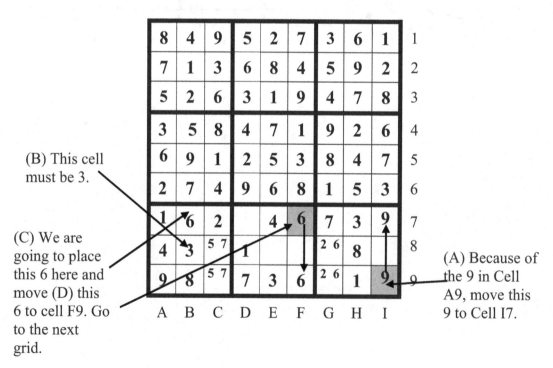

(B) This cell must be 3.

(C) We are going to place this 6 here and move (D) this 6 to cell F9. Go to the next grid.

(A) Because of the 9 in Cell A9, move this 9 to Cell I7.

## Grid 6

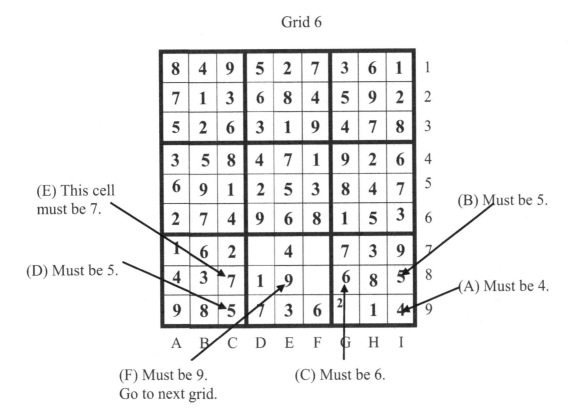

(E) This cell must be 7.

(B) Must be 5.

(D) Must be 5.

(A) Must be 4.

(F) Must be 9.
Go to next grid.

(C) Must be 6.

A  B  C  D  E  F  G  H  I

## Grid 7

(D) This cell must be 8.

(C) Must be 5.

(B) Must be 2.

(A) Must be 2.

A  B  C  D  E  F  G  H  I

The solution grid is now complete. The last step is to decide which numbers to take out to form a new Sudoku puzzle.

## In Closing

The Sudoku phenomenon has only been with us for a few years and is a relatively new form of mental exercise when compared with other types of puzzles and games, i.e. crosswords, chess, card games etc. We are, therefore, at this point in time merely scratching the surface when it comes to the overall possibilities for participation in its unique form of recreation.

In the future I predict there will be Sudoku clubs, Sudoku seminars and Sudoku competitions. I personally plan to promote and perpetuate all of these activities hopefully in the very near future.

This book has been a labor of love that has taken me more than three years to write. I particularly want to thank Kristin Gillenwater for her help in putting this book together. I also want to thank Margie Templeton for her superb advice and line editing, and my son, Sam Cecil, for his hands-on help in arranging the grids.

I hope readers derive as much pleasure reading this book as I had writing it.

*Jack Cecil*

## Blank Grids

Use the blank grids on the following pages to help you learn to solve Sudokus. Simply copy the clues from the newspaper or magazine onto these larger blank grids. They are easier to see and more durable than newspaper stock.

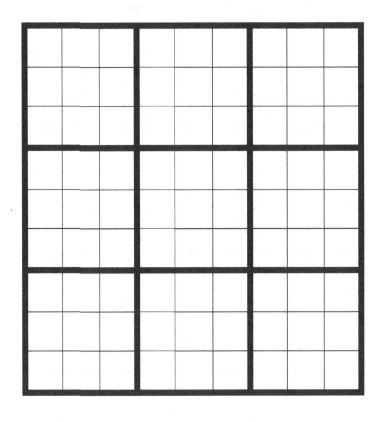

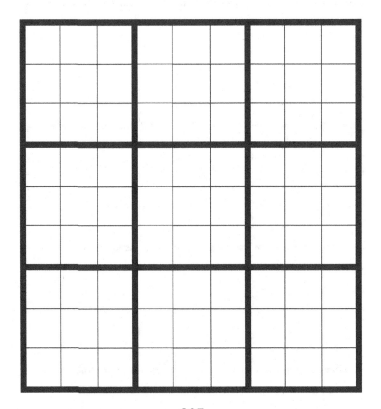

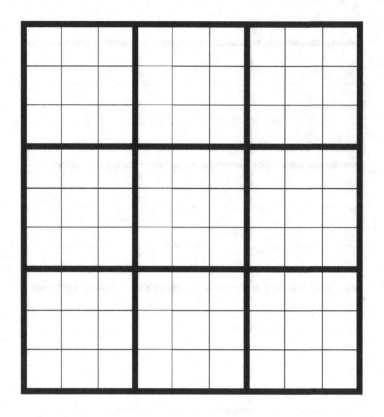

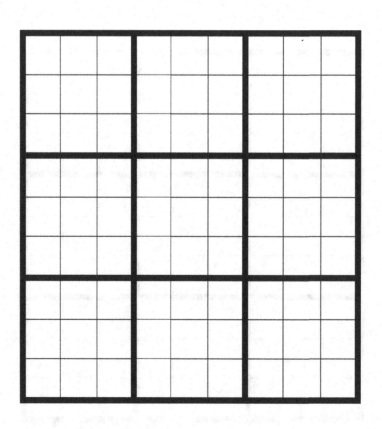

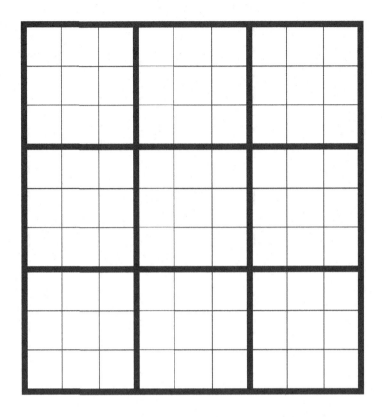

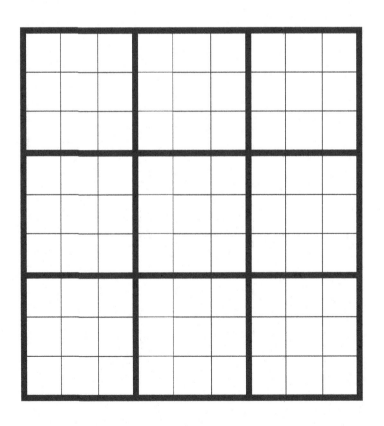

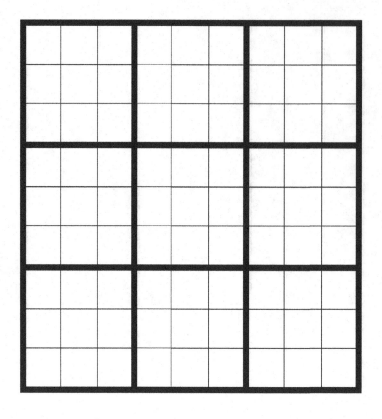

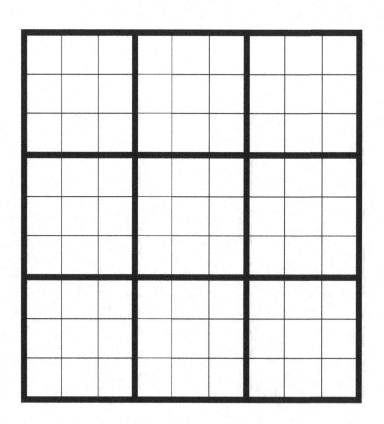

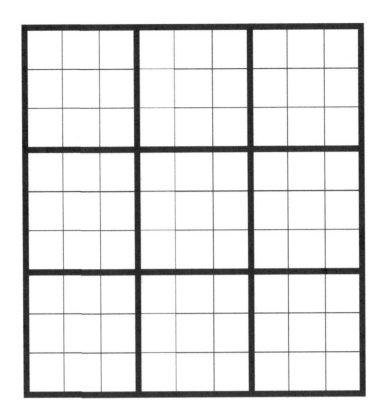

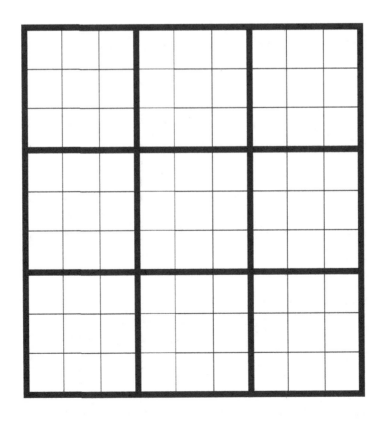

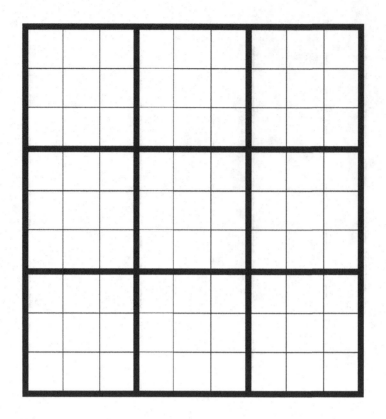

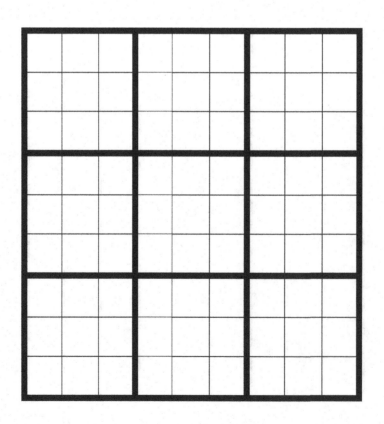

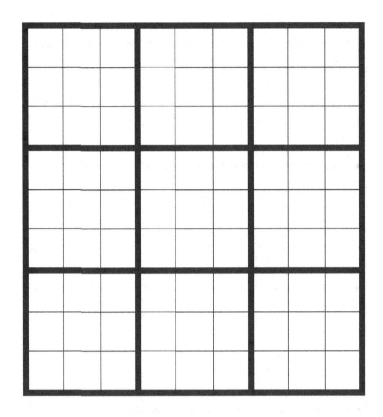

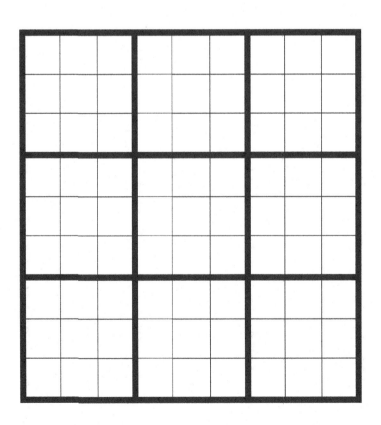

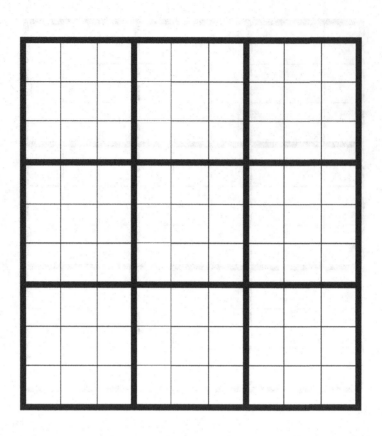

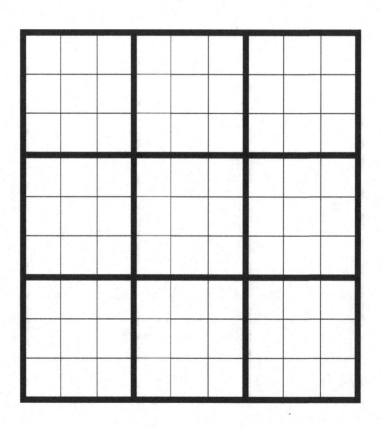